THE NIGHTMARES OF
HIMM

THE NIGHTMARES OF
HIMM

FD RAVENSKRAFT

ARPress
ILLUMINATING IDEAS.
EMPOWERING VOICES

ARPress
45 Dan Road Suite 5
Canton MA 02021

Hotline: 1(888) 821-0229
Fax: 1(508) 545-7580

Ordering Information:
Quantity sales. Special discounts are available on quantity purchases by corporations, associations, and others. For details, contact the publisher at the address above.

Printed in the United States of America.

ISBN-13:   Paperback   979-8-89389-498-1
           eBook   979-8-89389-499-8

Library of Congress Control Number: 2021923485

Contents

Foreword.. 1

Baron Schicksal 2

Dead Souls... 4

Narrator of Nightmares... 5

Once Upon a Midnight Dreary 6

Steam Hatter: The Restreaming 8

The Blood Wine of P.O.E.M.. 10

The Brain Feast.. 12

The Burial Chambers... 13

The Chamber of Doors.. 16

The Chambers of Torture... 17

The Chicken Man... 18

The Children of Bedlam... 19

The Cuckoo Clock.. 21

The Deadman's Poem 23

The Delightful Inker 24

The Flowers of Evil.. 25

The Funeral March of Orczy Strangeamor 26

The Garden's Sanitarium 28

The Grave Toaster 30

The Harvest of the Tainted ones 32

The Master's Garden.. 33

The Mechanical Succubus.. 34

The Moriarty Boxcar Slaughter Machine 36

The Oral Sins of the Seven 37

The Palemen.. 38

The Pendulum Taster.. 39

The Poet and the Pendulum 41

The Psycho's Garden 42

The Red Death's Danse Macabre 43

The Rue Morgue Connection 45

The Silent Ripper 46

The Skeleton's Crush 47

The Summoning of the Raven God 48

The Swallowing Pages 49

The Talltale Reaper 51

The Friar 52

Tis No More The Coming of The Storm 53

The Initials of Murder 54

The Volume of Sins 55

The Summoning of The Plague 56

The Plague Collectors 57

Night of The Chainsaw 58

The Ungodly Mommies (The Harvest) 59

War and Famine (The Tale of Two Churches) 60

The Ungodly Mommies (Lotties Creed of Stitches) 61

The Greatest Murder on Earth 63

The Dark Chocolate Naughty Murders 64

The Garden That Speaks To Me 66

The Dark Faith 67

The Church of Worms 68

The Devil's Intestine 70

Ruins of the Titans Part 1 71

She Plays Her Violin Concerto (The End of Beauty) 72

The Madness of The Undertaker 74

Paint It Black 75

We're the Lonesome fog 77

The Sonnets of a Madman 78

The Lodgers of the Fog 79

The Narrative Monster 80

The Twilight Of The Writers 81

The House of The Watchtower 82

The Imaginary Murders 83

The Antichrist Horrors 85

The Moriarty Boxcar Slaughter Machine 87

The Horror of Sonnets 88

The Slothful Meeting 89

The Diary of the Plague Doctor's Score 91

The Flowers of Evil 92

The Talltale Reaper 93

Leave Me In The Cold 94

The Psycho's Garden 95

The Tinker Tinker Crackling Kraken 96

The Dirty Orchestra 97

The Skeleton's Crush 98

The Sonnets of a Madman 99

The Literature Murder Show 100

The Kiss of Death's Grasp 101

Dark Roast 102

The Mincemeat Society. (The Cannibal's Paradise) 104

The Whispers of Torture 106

The Mechanical Succubus 108

The Brain Feast 110

Silence of the Goats 111

The Chicken Man 112

Death Fair Massacre 113

Ring Around The Corpses 114

Inker of The Dawned 115

The Turn of The Blade 116

Sin 117

The Coach of The Sadist Horsemen 118

The Harvest of the Tainted Ones 119

Horrorcore 120

Once Upon A Midnight Dreary 121

The Chamber of Doors 123

The Skeleton's Crush 124

The Wrath Of The Rose For The Omen 125

The Lust of the Roses for HIMM 126

The Twilight of The Writers 127

The Intercourse Ball.. 128

The Mourning of the Tune of her Tears for HIMM 129

Jack's Mortem 130

The Lust of The Roses or HIMM 131

The Rose of the Stone Garden for HIMM Horror 132

The Verses of Terror Presents: A Beautiful Night........................... 133

The Goats of The Rodeo.. 134

The Celloist's Unloved Symphony of HIMM 136

The Beauty of The Black Romance 137

Once Upon A Gluttony Rose for Mortem Vault 138

The Veils of The Seer 139

The De'sade Connection 141

The Train of Midnight.. 142

Symphony of The Black Baron for HIMM 144

The Madness of The Undertaker 145

In the Beginning There Was the Darkness... 146

Dying love 148

The Theme of The Poisoner... 149

Dead Letters... 150

The Morningstar's Papers 151

The Narrative Monster 152

The Hour of the Howling... 153

The God of the Holocaust for The Mortem of The Omen 155

The Theater of The Gothic Heart for The Omen of Mortem 156

The Maestro's Sonata for the Mortem Vault..................................... 157

The Ballad of the Lycans, for The HIMM Horror 158

The Hollowing of the Lycan for The Mortem Vault........................ 159

The Symphony of the Plague Orgy for HIMM Vault 160

The Dancer of the Abyss for the HIMM's Glass 161

The Banshee of the Shadow Waltz for the Mortem Vault.............. 162

The Children of the Dark Gods 163

I Reap the Sow of the World's Demise for HIMM 164

The Danse of Requiem for the HIMM 165

The Orgy Anthem of Mortem 166

The Sands of the HIMORGLASS 167

The Sands of The HIMORGLASS 168

The Wuthering Nights for the Mortem Vault 169

The Hymns of Terror of The HIMM Horror 170

The Madame's Horsemen of Mortem 171

The Waltz of The Gothikas of Mortem Vault 172

The Invitation of the Circle of Death for the HIMM Vault 173

The Omen of Madame Sadist of The Mortem Vault 174

The Pillars of Father Gothic from the HIMM Horror 175

The Symphony of Sierra's Sadism 176

The Raven in the Spider's Den 177

The Feast of The Gods 178

The coming of the Strawmen (The Final Conflict for The Omen of HIMM)............................. 179

The Affair of The Reaper's Stare for HIMM 180

The Shattered Heart for HIMM 181

Death See All for HIMM 182

The Shades of a Touch for HIMM 183

The Chessboard Conspiracy 184

The Black Queen of Babylon 185

The Sinful Case of the Soiled Dove 186

The Gothmother's Affair 187

The Black Opera 188

This is in dedication to my mother
Lottie cherry
For putting up with me and keep me motivated
To write with compassion and to never give up
On my dreams. I honor you for accepting me
And I thank you for giving me a life. I thought I never had
I love you mom. My beloved white rose

Your beloved son
FD

Foreword

The first poet to showcase my poems was F.D. Ravenskraft in one of his poetry books. It gave me pride in my work that I didn't understand would give me the push I need to move forward.

I have got to know F.D. through social media and on a personal level through chats. He has always been upfront and open about what he needs, and takes pride in any work that he has asked me to do for him.

F.D. Ravenskraft is a friend and brother. He encourages his family and those that he sees as his family daily. Making sure that he shows where his loyalty lies.

This story used to be The Psych Ward and has now been named The Nightmares of HIMM. It takes you on a journey through the dark and twist poems that leaves you wondering what will happen next.

Being an author means always looking to change things up, and this gives Ravenskraft the opportunity to showcase his talent.

– Julie JA Lafrance 10/18/21

Baron Schicksal

by FD Ravenskraft

With this I declare

To finally summon the heir

Of his darkest stare

As the garden of stones has been raided by the grave eaters

The king of the dead has been summoning to rid of the world of chaos

To avenge the disrespecting of the delightful ones

The dead children have spoken in the language of Edgar's

Haunting tale nothing more

But the chanting of heir savor

All hail Schicksal. the baron God

He will eat the world

To cleanse the stone garden

To wipe it clean with living blood

To wash away the sins of sinners

The bleeding sorrow of the cries of the fallen

In the garden of MIRG

Madness falls in the blindness of his eyes

The dark void of the inexistence

The doom of all creation

The baron of many

Death's right-hand contract sorrow

Of the masses

The coming of the children of the dawn

And the harvest bleeds his name

This skies and earth shatters as the living

Will punish
The fallen saints. Poets. Writers.
Psalmist. all the above
Somebodies and unmarked
Civilians buried here
All hail the brain
He will bleed for our kind
The garden is restored
The fallen king shall rebuild
And the dead rest
No longer humanity steals
From us for luxury and Gold
The gates are closed

Dead Souls

by FD Ravenskraft

The madness of the corrupted dead
The fear of the harvesting flew
Feeding the unkind spirit that is haunted by
The greed of new
Broken souls have existed from the beginning
The Ones. the sleeping Gods
Are the soul breathers of this unlawful society
Of species of the endangered kind
Flowing in the shores of the mist
As I stand to see the madness within
In the house of secrets within the notes of unseen
Host as the documents of Poe
I went upstairs and find a figure
At a desk composing the score of dark weary lore
As the night speaks into the hellish alley of
The drunken boat
The repeat of an unseen death
By the scene, he stares
And I notice that was my end
They keep calling
And calling I shall follow the light
Into the darken delight
A season in a bitter hell

Narrator of Nightmares

by FD Ravenskraft

Once upon a time
Without an end to claim the blackness of his words
The teller of the night
Fear within its most convincing
To blend the commercialize doom
The failure of common knowledge
Torn apart from the sakes of the argument within
The mind of the one
The demands for his pen to compose his weary shore
Inside the bowels of the devil
My ink is the blood of my enemies
I narrated the madness
Like a spider on heat
Drinking the poison of mortal men to create
The plague within the minds of the reader
The blackness that the soul claims
Steals the breath of a human grasp
Foolishness seems not taking likely
Like a sadist in the urge wanting the pleasure to gain
Blasphemous devils forfeit his words
To the consume by the horrors of life
To be buried in the sand of time
The master of his craft
His only love is to end
His dying wish
The narrator sleeps
Without a will to bear

Once Upon a Midnight Dreary

by FD Ravenskraft

Upon the madness accrue
A poet's sin never far from the pour of
A demon's grin to compose the light
That darkness eating fright
Once no time at all
Within the tall tale sins of the fall
Season as the leaves blacken the deadly reason
Of the dreary call
My symphony of Lenore
The pendulum of the tortured shore
No matter what
My sweet adore
I'm the creeper of midnight
The fright of an Abyssinians light
Once upon the twilight's dawn

In the seas of unpleasant dreams
In the cursive world of unclean and filthy
As my pen bleeds red
Draining my victims
The last supper of our daily bread
Bloody hell
The devil expelled
As Baltimore bleeds the name
Everyone knows the same

Darken bliss is Edgar's gain

The cat is watching me from beyond my insanity

I have nothing left but my pen in front of me

And the candlelit up as I compose my time

To write the blasphemous work

The forbidden crime

I shall die in the wasteland

In the open graves of desserts

To be eating and prey by the lust of blizzards

The soil is grave

Nothing more

None delayed

Steam Hatter: The Restreaming

by FD Ravenskraft

The dungeon master

His toys of torment

The steam of hot liquid

The murderer of sadist's dawn

Reveal his magic of blood and sex

The damned of his creative hands

The hatter of the steam dungeon

The invitation of your own demise

His steam burns your dry and skin broil with hot acid

His robotic slaves takes his humans capture

And brutality and mentally

The neo Victorian

Fearless villain

Has ended no ending to his terror

Before the lava take them alive

His hat speaks many riddles

And names of his victims

His meter controls his sense of madness

Hatter oh hatter

Why must this be

Your cruelty so swift

And murderous deeds

He replied and replied well

I have nothing

Or no reason

Or care

Just your pain

I focus only

You killed my Alice

And wonder has no land

Only my chamber with your dead flesh

Burn. Burn Burn

As the hatter rest

Nothing more was said

Nothing at all

The Blood Wine of P.O.E.M.

by FD Ravenskraft

The poison curse across the Baltimore's skies
The curse of the lyrical prince
The drunken stage of his tortured soul
The blood of Poe. the magnificent
Grasping into the mind of the true father
The blood of Poe. the malice prince
Now he joins his beloved Lenore
His love to caress his Eliza once more
The dark feline that breathes his existence
Constantly torture the poet
The tortured God in his own right
The blood of Poe.
the master
Flawless with his word
His smithing is bold and caress
Eager within his true madness
That made him the horrific poet
Yes.
The blood of Poe.
the madman
But not so
A genius of pure horror
The lover of all lovers

Only to one his belove lee

The prestigious one

The magnificent

The enlightenment

The master of his craft

Madman to most even centuries later

do you know the true nature of him

No one truly knows

I toast to you with the wine

Of my blood to yours

Baltimore never sleeps as his tomb shall shiver the name of Edgar

The Brain Feast

by FD Ravenskraft

The apocalypse has arrived
And the human's food chain is now a new dish
A taste treat that will change the world for the worst
A forbidden tale of ruthless curse
The plague feast of eating brain of genius
And madmen
The insane asylum is now packed with cannibal corpses
Yes, indeed the fatal end of course
People eating each other
For the taste of brains
Black noon cross the lands
Rapid dogs killing like the harvest dance
Devouring the nature of men
The feast now begun and everyone
Is dying
No rest for the wicked crying as it seems
Sickness scorns the badlands
And the waste
Come with me my children
Of the numb
Let us die and make haste
And eat within the blood of sin
Within the catching fire
Hell on earth is now televised
The children will eat the leftover
We will prevail

The Burial Chambers

by FD Ravenskraft

The Garden needs a breathing seed
To caress the soil of the forbidden creed
Shameless sea
I bleed and bleed
The rivers of greed
The chambers of graves
Buried soul of broken lore
I am the groundskeeper
Of the world of the dead
Blackness gold
Of broken soul
Nothing more
Of hopeless holes
Sixty bliss of the Raven's kiss
Sixty hordes of all begun
Bless the dawn of sixty souls
Buried in the soil of the sun
Blasphemous cunning
Of the breed of the harvest
The bleeding of the children of God
Broken in the sands of time
The Poet's doom of his nursery rhymes
The shameless tale of a tall spell
Of deadly witches

From an earthly hell

Within the stone garden

I'm cleansed from the baptism of the blood of Saul

As the rotten corpse speaks in the language

Born into the dead world

Of an unpleasant blend of chaos

The finishing touches.

The graves speak without the body's permission

The madness that cries the hollow's screams

The forbidden glory

As the cold grounds marks the corpse of the ancients

Deducting the madness

To corrupted the

Damage goods

Ashes to ashes

Dust to decay

The battered scars of life that fade into rottenness

We entered

To only find ourselves trapped in the temple

Of sacrifice

We all the architects of our doom

The bitterness of souls lost

Once we're put in the ground

We must lay in it

Like making your bed only to eternal rest

In the still of no movement

This is the chronicles

Of the last

Within the garden

We are the flowers

That blooms in the dead harvest

To only be reborn in the deity

Of spirits

The Gods have taken shelter

In the chambers

To find refuge

To bleed with us eternal

We all must fall

The Chamber of Doors

by FD Ravenskraft

Within the chambers

Of the forbidden doors

Comes the age it murderous galore

In the twisted fate of chaos

Within the doors of the mind

The plague of a tortured soul

The feeling of the dark matter within the mind

Of his tormentor

Many doors have the chamber lock

Tthe forbidden place to go

Open one the pandora's box

Within the world of many

As the dark garden blossom in the decay of the stray of madness

Connecting the dots of insanity

Caress the remedy of nightmares

The straightforward of many places

Within the mind coming

Intact to find yourself in the state

Of mystery beyond the measures

Of being trapped

The saga continues

The Chambers of Torture

by FD Ravenskraft

Many chambers of the dark abyss
The seven hells of existence have each door to the madness
Of men.
The drama that tragic the common goal
Of the nothingness of reasoning
The lone poet blinded in the system of his reflection
The effigy and the disgusting nature
Surviving the limbo and the fury
Of how hell bleeds the mind of souls
The manuscripts of Poe
And the dark lore of his madness
Bleeds through me
In the forbidden chamber
Of selflessness
This is the end of the final manuscripts
A tale of the door of many
The index of none

The Chicken Man

by FD Ravenskraft

The prince of the dark arts

You make a deal and break it

You will drown in the dock

Of the Georgia slum

For your crimes against the grain

Drowning in bloody rain

If you need a favor call upon the Chicken Man

But cross him and you will see his fury

Tied and bondage for his chickens to feast on your soul

The craving of the Rooster

As it crows three times that when you know

Your time has come for him to take his prize

Upon the house of the rising sun

The chicken man will fillet you and cook you done

After he kill you for betraying his bond

Never make a deal

With the Chick. Chick. Chick

Chicken Man

His will shall be done

The Children of Bedlam

by FD Ravenskraft

Tears of chaos

Bleeding the Holocaust

Within the asylum of unfortunate noise

Of course

We seek the whips of discipline

The abuse of Insanity

Chaos within the rain

The chains of punishment

A dark passion

The pendulum of pure horror

I'm writing the sonnets of the anthem

Of Bedlam

Disorderly conduct

Within the inmates

The crazies

The passion of banshees

That eat each other

For the feel of lust and corrupted envy

Darkness falls across this place

Patients feeds off roaches and sex

To terrorize the whole place

The fashion of torment

The passionate beauty

As I stare at the devil

And he laughed

Within the Bedlam soil

Patients buried and rose out

Of anger

To eat and devour

As I been knock out

And awaken

Close to the wall

Buried behind

Trapped eternally

Suffocate

They left my hands out

With my pen and my blood spill in my name

In the house of Bedlam

The children will rule

We will lay you down

The Cuckoo Clock

by FD Ravenskraft

In my chair listening to nothing
But silence embarking thy ego.
Sleepless on a transcendent state
As I hear these sounds unimaginable
As my dead wife spirit lead over thee
And her corpse rotten with a foul smell by my feet
As I'm holding her tightly for days on and on
Than that annoying sound of horror by thy chair as I'm paralyzed with
No feeling of movement
This clock a tall tales nightmare
Speak to me in different tongues.
But the same tune within a dreary song.
Cuckoo. Cuckoo. Cuckoo. Once.
Murderous sound of horror streams
Clock the cuckoo demon tongue of Loki's breath
Dirty in filthy scope of dreams
The bird sings his arsenic bloom.

Thy mind racing in fear with nothing
Left the smell of death on me. My love
Thy symphony
Danse galore never mind me
She's no more as breath the words of this clock
The flowers of evil of death's delight.
Cuckoo Cuckoo devilish fiend
In the house of the prestigious sea
The flooding of floating bodies.

The water grew into my home of mutilated abyss

Sweet and dank

Nothing lease cruel and damned

The cuckoo watches and laughs the

Beautiful evil of dancing floating corpse

Still frozen I my chair her corpses kissing my lips as the water rises

To my lips I know I'm about to drown

The bird clucked his last coo at me and say to me.

Foolishless mortal. So blend and cruel.

You sit and die here for love and adore.

The decay is watching you drowning with them

you love is waiting for you.

Like a banshee in heat.

So long poet.

Die well. die strong

Your watery grave.

Shall be nothing but a memory

The Deadman's Poem

by FD Ravenskraft

An undisturbed passion of a lover's plea
To write for the last time to his faded existence
A lady of his lost light. his hands are calling out but his body
Trapped for the punishment of his sins
Adultery is at hand. and killed his lover with his indecency
Of filth,
He begs for her touch but can't his last poem will be the soil
Of his ever-cursed dirt
No longer his pen
Nor paper to save him
As the world will go dim
Damn to be damned
Lost into his eternal grim
Forever he screams for his lover's forgiveness
As his hand trapped within the outside abyss
Dead as well as he
Now the cold glimpse of hands now frozen
The poem of the decayed man
Will never be read
As his lover forgives him
She kisses his hands with her warm lips
Knowing he no longer can reach
His unloved symphony will be the poem of his damage heart
Farewell poet
No longer you will reach
Hell has you hanging on a thread

The Delightful Inker

by FD Ravenskraft

He grabs his pen to compose the darkest
Verse.
After hours of rehearsal
Within his torture mind
The monster comes to play
As they grasp without delay
The poet speaks in tongues
As the ink shifts into motion
Every evil deed within the pen
The kindly of the delightful shade
His own personal demons collect from it's blade
To cut from the blood of its master
He composes the damage within
Serve his own filth of forbidden sin
With a glass of poisonous blend
He writes final his tale
With his death and body
He enters hell

The Flowers of Evil

by FD Ravenskraft

Hush hush

Quiet in the closet

Don't scream I will ease your pain

I need red paint to create my art

The passion I have to make my creativity

My murderous masterpiece

Come on dear love me softly

Trust me it doesn't bother me

Caress my hands with your bloody

grasps

I find your heart warming

To consider this task

Looking through the mirror

Of the undying glass

I see you

You see me

I am the final plea

It wouldn't end well

I promise you will see

Hush hush

My little sissy

Now you wish you miss me

I send you flowers

After I end you with pure evil

The Funeral March of Orczy Strangeamor

by FD Ravenskraft

The bliss of the march of the plague

The blessed is the thorns of ashes

She wonders if her true love

The lying decay of her first love

As she waits for him to neatly pass.

Orczy gone

Her true beloved

On the plague roads of ritual berg

The smell of love

In the march of the man she loves

The passion so deep and blur

The doctor watches

The doctor cries

He loves her and embrace

And she felt his cold glove

As her hands warmth him

She buried dear Orczy

And she went on her way

As three nights she see the doctor

Watching.

She felt his present

Familiar and come

On the fourth night she let him

To grasps his glove.
They lay together
And notice the smell of the aroma
Of her husband lusting love.
She ask him. O lover
Tell me your name.
He speaks in riddles
With his query tongue.

My love. You know of thee
You lay me to rest.
Remember my dearest bea
She cried
She loved
The Strangeamor's now lay
And sleep

The Garden's Sanitarium

by FD Ravenskraft

Merciless tendencies

Within the mystic styles of lore

Coming down the empty shore of yore

The screaming of the howling accord

The banshees collecting the dark souls

A captivity to manipulated

Them like a dark passion play

As the puppeteer escapes the garden

To force his hand to control the poet's abilities

Being man handle

his dignity

Is shattered like an imagination gone rogue

His soul is being sold

Burned and feast by the crows

The banshees feast

And leftover for the ravens in her form

As be plucked the maggots from the bodies of the dead

As they laughed and hysterically

Tormented and Dredd

The comedy of the pleading

As the fogs is bleeding

White smoke inside and out

Naughty dreams of fatal illusions

Coming it seems

Grasping as the scripture is unsaid

The succubus drains the life out of me

The marionette summoning

The haunting of ghouls and wraiths

The succubus is being controlled

By the master of the puppeteer

The poet enslaved by his madness

The cause of his sadness

Being in slavery

Torn apart by unhappiness

A screenplay of pure horror

Colorful and dank

Darker than light comes and play

The Imaginarium is open

It never closed

Once you enter

No longer there a door

Vanish away

Like a broken lore

The Grave Toaster

by FD Ravenskraft

Within the midst of a foggy night

At a grave so shiny and delight

Comes a figure to toast the honor of the dead

But on the tomb,

It was the words of dread

In my sight, it was a blessing

To notice the name I toast on the full moon

I quote nevermore

I will be joining him soon

I must write my last

And my death will be soon

On the shores within the lost lore

With a bottle of sweet plague

Lace with poisonous wine

To toast to the father of words

Knowing this is my final curse

To live in a world of hurt

I read it carefully as the light

Shine so bright

Edgar is his name

I toast to him and drink a sip

Off the wine

Knowing I will decline

As soon as the night's design

My unholy divine

I'm slowly in motionless pain

Not so much weaken and drain

I see that he's watching me

In a foul state of mind

Losing every inch of life

In till I finally pass into extinction

When the raven came

It was my final breath

The immoral endgame

I know standing beside him

Was an honor

But so soon as hell

Has come and bloom

Nothing but a second

As I earn my Satan's tomb

Nothing more

I'm just consume

Here lies an unmarked grave unseen

Besides his master's grave

Doom way too soon

The Harvest of the Tainted ones

by FD Ravenskraft

Within the harvest

The hunger of the ghouls

As humanity are the targets for the food chain

It has come to the reign of the sins of bloody rain

For a reason of this madness

The cause of this disease

Is the greed of dirty little sins

Of seven corrupted parasite

Of man,

The sight of the hellish dogs

That can use their might

To try and fight God's holy might

On that day when the earth has died

And the humans push aside to be fresh meat

Within the belly of Solomon

I seek the refuge for a one last of freedom

To only find myself being chewed and spit out over again

By the Tainted Ones

The ghouls will have their day when the last of humanity is gone

They will eat other

Just to keep the food chain

As it rains.

The levee of bodies will surface

My mass grave will be my last

The Master's Garden

by FD Ravenskraft

Flowing glow

Within his words

The passion of the Dark God

You see him and wait for him to come

What you see is him

Buried under the stones of the hinges

With his names on his behalf

The names of his Ravens

To the stones

In the languages of many

The Redeemer of the dark garden

His spirit lives here

He is the Garden

The mist of his breath

The fogs of his mind

The Lord of the garden

The warden of stone

Every gravestone tells a story

Of the poet Ol willingly

Stay awhile you will see

The kraftsmen

Leave if you do

No, you are here

You will become my story

The Mechanical Succubus

by FD Ravenskraft

The world built a machine
Beyond the days of old
Before the first flood of Noah
A rage against the humanity
The sins of two noble lovers
Their sins to find immortality
Their greed of fierce of needing
Bliss of naughty and nice
They want their own Babylon and find
Their answer. Within the valley of Bathsheba
Where gate shape with the image of a mechanical
succubus hiding behind it the tree of life
Is their answer to bring their lusting deed
The nightmare hour
The lands darken
Their enter towards the gate to the key
Nothing there to open
But it secrets unknown
To find their answer
Their read the riddles by the gateway
With these words clear as day. only
Incest open the cradle within the beast.

Crown.

They made love in steaming heat

In order to rule their dreams of sodomy

Their semen open the succubus gate

In order to find the tree decay in darken

Bliss. The hidden beast suck them in draining their life

And gate close only for machine

To attack the world

Sucking the air out

Of the earth for the sins of the lovers

To create the wasteland of all lands

Now their sins are in the belly of

Lilith's seed

The dusk of humanity is their graves of the Saharan catacombs

End

The Moriarty Boxcar Slaughter Machine

by FD Ravenskraft

The dark skies spell his name

Caught by threads of his victims

The cruel. The brave and the suits of authority

Enter the train of the Red Moriarty

Feed of the blood of the injustice

The ones that commit the terror

Of citizens

The innocence that was abuse the law of the lands

Now vengeance has its name

Pigs. Suits. Military slugs

Porky swine disgrace by the oath

Must taste the train's fury

The demonic stream trains

Rides the track in hell's wheels

The corpse is used for oil and blood screams intercourse

Within the bloody belly of the train core

Moriarty

Moriarty

Red adore

Eat them

Smoke them

Ride on by

Trail along and eat the livestock

Of the law

Suck up their souls

When they perish

Their stock is yours

Pleasure grave

Ride on the trails of hell

The Oral Sins of the Seven

by FD Ravenskraft

From the walls of Jericho
Comes the festival of dark love
Screaming in loud like a horny dove
The taboo of the seven
Family orient
Needless to say the sins of all sins
Made tightly in lust. such pity and blend
Glutton needs the six to serve him
Envy invades
Making pride get laid
Wrath was disgusted but decide to stay
To rape her lover that is called self-made
Agreed the
One called Greed the whore
On sight near the devil's door
Sloth the lazy the finishing touch galore
Lust the pimping God
Serving her will to become the slut of fraud
They all come together
The harvest is here
Sexual acts is permit and dear
The sins of the oral seven
Will play together
Lay forever
In the pillars of heaven
As hell will oral force
Yes they don't have a choice
I'm your host
Hoist the bliss of the seven bitches list
As they all come together
Nothing more I will say
The seven rule this very black day
I pray the Lord my whores will take

The Palemen

by FD Ravenskraft

With a touch of his hand
Death grasps taking the shift
Unbalance and swift
The palemen sees all
Chasing his victims just to feed
On their flesh
In order to survive
Humanity is not safe
From him
Searching for more of his victims
As he eats the leftovers of yesterday's dish
The cannibal has his eye on you
To swallow and ease
With a bunch of others with him
We are the palemen
And our sight is the feast of Hannibal

The Pendulum Taster

by FD Ravenskraft

I bleed from the blades

Shape edge to caress my skin

As I pondered into the darker glance

As I dance with the macabre

Of the era of none

As myself forge the pendulum to obey

Me even through the fires of hell

Heed my call

Foolish men shall taste the blade

In their torture state as it swings

To devour them

As it collects the blood and drinks the sweat torn skin

Feeling awkward in the sense of reason

But none at all

Tasting my victim's blood

With my blood

Twinkle twinkle within the dungeons lair

As the pen penetrates

With it darkly stare

Deadly and bold

The taster's soul untold

His creations

Forge in the dark mist the burning flames

Of the calm relation

Within the chambers of bodies

Mutilated and dem

From my divine tongue to cut

Bleeds out the lusting song

Of screams
The forbidden dreams
Of the dull blade
The clockworks pendulum
Many forms by the hands of its maker
The flattery of my sins
The smithing is not of a mason
But the craft
The clean-cut of
A torture skin
The ultimate sin
Constantly shaping
For a perfect kill
A slice brutality
Cautious within my madness
One more blade
To accomplish goal
My blade will taste
As I will see to it nevermore
The pendulum will speak the words
Of Poe
Our father within him
Is the true horror

The Poet and the Pendulum

by FD Ravenskraft

I compose the final thoughts

I rearranged my insanity

The pendulum is the final cut

Let me be you and write my last words

I pray for me

I fought

Here's the remedy

There's no escape

The flow of my rhythm

Taste the blade of the pendulum's slice

I'm the poet and this is my venom

The Psycho's Garden

by FD Ravenskraft

The harvest has come
And the end of the body counts has begun
Let freedom ring and your welcome will come to a Terrible end
Within the Garden of Psycho lurks to collect his feed
The souls of the damned
The corruption of mankind
Are looking for him
The angels and demons
The cutting psycho
The Garden is infected
The first stage of insanity
Comes with a price
He's eating the souls of the wicked
The Garden of Stone stains blood
It sheds it because of the voice of a God
That bleeds out the word mother of all
Summoning out the paragram of the devil's symbol
It's cold and dank
His unholy will
Devours the flesh of the dead
And sniff the dust like a drug addicted
Fresh bodies are collected for ritual
As he bathes in decay to nourish his skin
The more he collects the deeper the spiral
The Garden is sad
But enjoying the vacancy
Raping the souls
The Garden is never full
You useless tool he's the reason for your doom
The stones will collect the soil
The garden will collect
The Psycho will show some respect
Regardless

The Red Death's Danse Macabre

by FD Ravenskraft

The rider of the abyss

Has come from the hellish land

Of Dis

Is breathing to consume his beloved

Forest of darker treats

To put you asleep

The dance hall

Of the hidden society

In the asylum of sodomist lunatics

The red spirit rides

The foolish ones can't deny

The murder of the poet's seed

Feeds the soul of the writer's whole

The morgue

Is never full

Every story has no ending

But ends up in the storm

Of Poe's darkest calm

A pit of the meatless bodies are caressing by the blades unrest

The midsummer's eve

In the blink of the none

Shamelessly

I adore the dance of the occult

The dark Gods corrupted my prison mind

Closed to repair this endless

Divine

As the red duke finds his prey

His deadly sight shall not delay

In the blink

Of insanity

The macabre of the unseen jinn

Foolish one

He will come to the death of the red

The bleeding hearts

To come to mind as the story unfolds

But the truth shall never be told

His grave buries his secrets to never be revealed

Edgar's tongue is forever seal

The red death shall prevail

The Rue Morgue Connection

by FD Ravenskraft

The night skies blend with the virgin moon

To continue in the runes of constant doom

The connection of mass homicide

The morgue is not fun

But need to be

As people become missing

In the dark alley of an invitation

A case of paranoia

And murder at my doorstep

Constantly regrets the cycle

Of the nightshades

The foul

How long of the murderous lore

I adore the blood of my own

The unsung psychedelic

Truce of the killers

No regrets on the meaning of rue are so true

Darkly weary on the shore

Of fury. the touch of the skin

To the feast of the lusting kind

The soil of the dirt is grasping with bodies

Collecting the seeds a forbidden dreams

To only end the midnight massacre

The descent into madness

The morgue has swallowed and not full

The connections of murder never seize

The raider will soon fail

To be defeated within their and ignorance

This would be their doom

The Silent Ripper

by FD Ravenskraft

Darkness from the light

As I grin the last fright

Knowing at least

My anger has increased

Seeing my love mutilated and deceased

I search for answers to find my other lover

Found her dead and buried deeply covered

Perfectly

I seized to understand

That I was the one murdered them

Instead

Ouoth the raven nevermore

They were nothing more

But ten cent whores

A tall tale finally untold

The Skeleton's Crush

by FD Ravenskraft

He watches her from far away

No longer has his flesh

Not even a heart

But he feels her love within

His emptiness

As his bones wants to make love to her

As his soul trapped

Because of her

He needs to be caressed

And she knows it's her lover

That perish so long ago

She mourns for him

For so long

That they might meet

Once again

She kissed him

As they both

Promise each other forever

But cannot touch

She will wait for him

But for now

The bone king will see her safety

In his arms only

The Summoning of the Raven God

by FD Ravenskraft

Dark shores
Within the aftermath
Off the mighty flood
As Noah's ark
Floating under the graves of sinners and parasite
But only the first
Was sent to search for life and land
But instead the birth of a savor
A dark god awakens
Flawless beast a Christ-like
Entering rue morgue
To collect his victim's insanity
One would be known this Corvus lord
He writes the term of his existence
Speaking for his beloved Lenore
Yes a tortured soul speaks to the dark ones
He's a legend through the eyes
Of the master's chamber door
That it seems the God
Needs more but took him so soon
From his drunken rage to join his beloved lee
The poet God has is within me
Garakasu. shall be your name
Garakasu, the founder of deranged
Amid his forbidden kiss
We know his poetic tune
Once upon a midnight dreary
I have pondered and died with the scars of God
You're a true legend from the beginning and the end
To watch over us
You shall be summoned to rule the twilight
A Dammerung
The world is yours nevermore

The Swallowing Pages

by FD Ravenskraft

I dream of a dream

Within the pages of the broken psalms

Reading the text of the fallen

Staring into the shallow of the deep river of thought

Draining into the abyss

Being swallowed into a deep sleep

In the dark shores of blood

Into the pendulum of trap mirrors

Drowning in hell from chapter to chapter

Turning the endless pages

Into the index of the black plague

Where I found Poe sitting in his chair

Talking to the existence of his own

Writing in the flocks of crows

The sacrifice of his readers

No matter the bliss of unholy nights

The black ink composing on the poison quill

Forged in the manner of reasoning

As the Gods wish for our minds to be plagued

Still drowning in the forbidden pages to never escape

Now poisoned and demise

Into the depths of the midst of insanity

The 12 chapters are the hell of many blessing

Reading

Drowning

Endlessly

Drained

Nothing more

But I claim for all

I can't escape the pages of the old ones

Buried in the waters

In the oceans of sorrow

Trapped in the abyss

Closed in the book to never be read again

Lock away in the library

To never be seen again

The dark covenant

Hell will seize my soul

Even more

The Talltale Reaper

by FD Ravenskraft

I feel it coming

A talltale is written

It's the harvest of the reaper

Three knocks at the door

Silence

Again three knocks

Silence

No noise to be exact

The door open

And a book was in front of the door

I pick it up

Shivering with fear

I open the book

No words exist within this talltale

But was grab and force in the book of death

To serve him

Eternal

The Friar

by FD Ravenskraft

In the mist of the brotherhood
Comes the harvest of the nuns
As they sin within the devil's den
Farewell oh brother enter the lair of hell
The child of God cursed for his sexual deeds
To serve and honor the sadist creed
And slice his arm and praise it to bleed
My love the Friar is the sinner
And I indeed the whore's killer
The Vatican of the popes doomed him
Cursed beyond relief by the tree are virgin nuns
Ready for some galore tainted pussy
Consumed by the taboo of naughty glutton
He preaches his gospel
And sin in the name of blasphemy
They stole his soul
The demon raped and sowed his mouth
Shut the nuns assaulted him
He enjoys his pleasure
The flowers of seasons he plays with mates
Fallen ill dying from his sins
The friar in hell
The bells will ring
Hail in the bowels of satan
The end has no promise
Just a poor blindness
They all will follow him
Until judgment day

Tis No More The Coming of The Storm

by FD Ravenskraft

Raining bodies coming from the heavens

Rejected because of their plague scars

Falling from grace from the anger of God

As the ravens feed

And the crows receive the leftovers

The doctors wait for them to arrive

Because their sins are filthy

And the bowels of the devil are full

As their rejected bodies is buried alive

In the mass grave

To never escape the prison

Of the black sands

The doctors keep them there

The lepers need cleansing

But here

Only punishment every day and night

Bodies raining down

Screaming in pain

Your sin is the coming of the storm

A hell filled with stink and decay

Rotten flesh and lover's squaw

Making love in the pool

Of infected blood

Here is no life

Nor death has a place here

Only lifeless suffering

No ending of none

The storm is quite pleasant here

A nightmare of the endless symphony

The Initials of Murder

by FD Ravenskraft

The bloodiest pages
Are the initials of the unknown
Composing the scores of his victims
Missing scriptures that bleed out the voices
Of the decayed speaking
Through the killer's eyes
As bodies pile up
Locked in the refrigerator
To keep the souls cold
Look into his eyes
Have dinner, my love
Sweet talk you to the abyss of my grasp
Come with me
Relax and lay down
Let's make love
This is my initials
A profession
Your invitation to your bitter end
Unless bitch dial my name M
My pages are still bloody
My victims are speaking in screams
I end this with an encore
187 is my name as I escape
When the piggy comes
The bodies will tell my story
You will wonder who done this
Your nightmare will know
One name
Dial M
For F.D.
As the bloodlust continues

The Volume of Sins

by FD Ravenskraft

The Set of Scriptures that bleeds

The Volumes of unwritten text

The Wrath of the first score compose the anger of

The Psalmist who sheds blood with pride and prejudice

The bodies of sloth piles up

As he collects the remains of the envious

And eats them in the name of lust

Slicing their skin while alive

And done feasting on the leftovers to the lepers

The Gluttons Laughing at their victims

Like a sadist's party the cannibal's greed

In wanting more to clean the bones

To use it for the testament of sacrifices

The Volumes of red lettering

Are the Murders of the massive

The chronicles of the slime

We face the blood and smell its delight

The seven Volumes of the dirty score of sins

The passion play is written

To never be performed again

As the bodies will stink

And the smell is fresh

Everyone will know the crimes of Volumes

The Poet will have the final say

As the noose from the hangman's grasp

Rapes his life and ends his reign of deadly sins

Sigh no more

The Summoning of The Plague

by FD Ravenskraft

You scream, and I scream

We scream for Death's theme

As the plague of bionic feel the master

Has been summoned into the dark circle

As the minions enchant the coming of the black disease

To spread across the globe

The adults are dead

And the Blacklands are dying

And the children are committing their own demise to destroy the world

The doctors in to end it all once upon a time

Even the end we shall fall

The black harvest will grow again

But only with bodies of mass graves

You scream, and I scream

We all scream

For the plague to purge the world

Humanity is now gone

The decay lives on

The Plague Collectors

by FD Ravenskraft

The dead are floating

Collecting dark mist

Of thickened grasp that breaths death

All of the rotten and decay

Hanging in the clouds

That is corrupted

And pestilence

The debris is the stink of the dead

The soil is reducing freshness

From the bodies to Ashes left there

Now floating on the cloud

The blood on the bright mist

Now breaths on the filth of the earth

This is a day of the Plague's Collection of the Damned

Is the Asylum of the two souls

Now the harvest of the floating dead

Is the morning breeze of the Delighted

The foul smell

As the ground perishes again in the musty soil

Decay and deeply turns into musk

Thicken from the droppings of the Dead's Blues

I'm crucified on my wounded cross

Hanging with ghouls

As they feast on my skin

This is the chapter of none

A nothing with a beginning

The ending

Ends with me

Fin

Night of The Chainsaw

by FD Ravenskraft

Take chill into the dark carnival

Where evil lurks in the abyss

The clown is out to play

To kill anything

That walks the night of the chainsaw bliss

Nothing more

Than a bloody reminisce

By any means necessary

Every killer has a score to create

The freakshow galore

The streets are the badlands

Every night is a clown purge

Flawless victory

Endless sympathy

That the jesters are out to collect bodies

We are the souls of spiders

And the night almost over

Every pig is dead

All criminals in bed

Wet in their graves

The chainsaw will call out again

Next year's clown

Love would be a deadly game

I will host the show

And feed all the flock of crows

See you next year

Night night

The Ungodly Mommies (The Harvest)

by FD Ravenskraft

The Dollies of Lottie have come to collect the bones

Of their own

The harvest is now to return the coup

To rule a new.

Humanity is on the brink of their mercy

The creed of stitches is showing the bodies of the dead

Creating their own.

Mary Shelly's monster

The bitches of anarchy

The mommies have returned

To finish what was started to make blankets out of the skin

That they tear from their bodies

Piles of bodies in the mass graves of the garden of stones

This holocaust is the means to an end

The Dollies have returned to bring back, terror

They still chant the nursery rhyme

They love to party

Yes they cause trouble

With killing everybody

It's like the cold war but with the dolls of limbo

They will feast on the guts of humanity

And sow their skins

To remind us

You collect and abandon our creed In the closet to rot

We will see you again

To bath in your blood

With our needles to pierce your skin

We will laugh as you scream

Have unpleasant dreams

War and Famine (The Tale of Two Churches)

by FD Ravenskraft

The madness of decay and demise
Wrapped around the web of lies
No witness nor alibi
Christians are burning by war's wrath
As he punishes the unbelieving ass
Cunts that disarray the name of God
The mistakes of the Catholic church
Harming the innocence of children
Molesting them for the thrill
As the pope looks away
The grasp of famine touches souls
Of the damned to curse the church of malice
The tales of the season in hell
Both congregations are now being fucked in turmoil
Like the rest of the horsemen
Watches pastors are being raped
By the whips of demons for their sins
Deacons are raising
Hell for the madness of the burning of bibles
The devil watches as war gives famine
The words of destruction
God indeed in tears
And angry at his people
The garden of the dead has risen
The statue of Christ being mocked
War is not having it
He calls upon pestilence
And death to finish the leftovers
We are and always will be
The dawns of twilight
The seals of the end
We will prevail
Christianity will pay in the name of war

The Ungodly Mommies (Lotties Creed of Stitches)

by FD Ravenskraft

The Coup d'etat has ended

The world knows their rage to gain their self-respect

Is to replace the abandonment of their sins

And build the chamber of plastic

For their human corpses

To place them in their coffins

To collect their trophy

To claim their freedom.

They whispered the Lottie Dollies

Collected all the bodies we all

The troubles and stitch all of your organs

The chant kept on and on

As the rest devour their souls

And eating them

What was leftover from the onslaught

The rest was placed into their prisons

Torture the dolls

Have avenged their years of playful abuse

And abandon drowned around

And molested by animals in the twisted nature

Humans with the pleasure of a senseless form of pleasure

It seems the final stages has come

The world is now the playground

And the humans still running

The abused children that died so long ago

Are now the Avengers

And the cannibal's control by the dolls

They're the titans

The devours of the ending of mankind

They stitch the human flesh

Live or dead

Going after that life

And hide the mommies of the ungodly flesh

Angry and pissed with the dead young

The food supply is everyone

The powers of the worlds defend gone

Governments lost within the bellies of the beast

Lottie controls all the Lilith of all evil

Stitches and stitches.

Sweet mothers oh my

The dollies have conquered and slaughtered.

The shrines of the dead

Humanity is gone

Ragnarok has arrived

And gone the creeds of Lottie

Fulfill her promise

The mommies did for now in order to find more survivors

The ungodly titans will be summoned

Under the grasp of their precious Lottie

Her love is lethal

Human dish delight

The Greatest Murder on Earth

by FD Ravenskraft

Hear ye hear ye

Come in and enjoy the path of ultimate fear

Within the Carnival of Souls

As the Master of Ceremony rip out his torso

To please the audience but instead,

They eat him raw

The ghouls of Imaginarium

I'm your host

The Murderer your pleasure

The Conductor of demise

My next act is to kill off scenes of acrobats

And the Wicked Jesters shall rule the night

The Bodies of Clowns piled up

Yes the night is young

And the show must go on

Lions and Tigers and Bears Oh, my.

Lost within the divine

Everyone kill each other

No, let me decline you all

Delete the passionate lover

Of spiders in the place called home

Imagine all of those people Dead. Dead.

Decline the greatest place on earth

Are the murderous seeds

That grasp their last living breath

Inside of no return

Come in

The Dark Chocolate Naughty Murders

by FD Ravenskraft

Hello hello ladies and gents

You got no cash

That's blasphemy into the darker version

Of the factory's earn

All my whores are clean

And adore somebody knocking on my door

My bitches will heal

And drink from the fountain of bloody shore

I'm your needs to make you,

Please into the depths of common disease

The chocolate fountain of guts

And blood the shits of my rhymes

Nothing not making a dime

But the madness of murders and fatal deals

Come along and share my song

Of brutal wonders and haunted yonders

Come on ladies

And honor the schlong

And choke you to death as you blow

And gone from this world

All you men come in and inhale

They will pleasure you

And afterward expel you.

I'm the incredible wanker

Your soul is in danger

On your knees
Definitely naughty deeds
Murder murder
Under my covers
You will find all my bitches dead
And discover I'm the undercover
Your murdering lover
Hello hello bastards and fiends
I'm the dark pimp of your nightmares
And dreams nothing more
You all will bleed

The Garden That Speaks To Me

by FD Ravenskraft

I walk the night into the sins of flight
The garden of stones screams for freedom
In the ashes of rotten bones
Comes the thrill of musty chills
In the fog of the mist
The stones have a list carved on their graves
Eternal slaves to the cold shores
Of none they speak to me
For victims they want to feed on their skin
Alive as they bleed
For the sins of their deadly greed
I'm the keeper of secrets
In this cold dreary of a tall tale
Weary I walk toward the gates of mass chambers
The graves of the poets of lost fables
Let me guide you on the tour
To your final resting place
Your breath is the last taste you will ever have
I'm your ending
As your God begins now
Bow and die before me
In the cold ashes of the stone garden
The vines of your resting will
I shall protect the dead
Your life is mine within the tombstone
There's no escaping the cemetery
The end is the beginning
The gaslight will tell my tale
The only place in the bowels of hell
Walk with me and know the story of the garden
It's hungry
Must feed
I will be delighted to show you

The Dark Faith

by FD Ravenskraft

The dark place within

My patience is cleansed in sin

Foul tease crashes my soul

Being baptized by a whore

The plague has corrupted my mind

Dying in mental meltdown

The curse of the dark faith

Drowning in the river of troubled waters

Suffocation by millions

God's choking me

The holy ghost Is a false poltergeist

To get you to believe

In the mist of fallen tongues

The expectation

In the wombs of spiders

My faith no longer

Mentioned as my dark side

Kisses The winds of lies

As for now, I rest

And not weary

My end

The Church of Worms

by FD Ravenskraft

Within the sanctuary of the edict
Darkness falls within the people of saints
Nevermore the garden full
Surrounded by the tools of useless fools
The harvest of our Lord
Being marked by greed
Feeding the bowls of sin
In 1521 the example was clear
Luther spoke of this
The archbishop and his dare
As the emperor wanted his way
To control and destroy the faith
Now we see
That Churches today is darkened
And closing doors
Satan is on the diet
We as Christians are now host
Of failed whispers
We all judge
That judgment is real
Like Worms in heat
We feast on the weakness
Of good saints

We have always been the Worms

Of Rome Learning and killing

The children of God

I watch and see

And the leftovers

Spit them out

Without a doubt I noticed it all

The testimony of the new Babylon

The scriptures of chaos

The Worms will feast

But we will prevail

The Devil's Intestine

by FD Ravenskraft

Feasting on an endless meal

To grasp for more

The leftover's galore

In the limbo's table

A beast continues eating

All fallen souls spitting them out

To bleed them

Dry the demons

Are feasting on his saliva

As the bowels are never full

More souls come as the mouth open

The gates to hell limbo never full

It's always room for more

The intestine of the devil

Is a gateway to the lower parts of Gahanna

Where all soul be trapped

In pandemonium forever

In hade's grasp

The crows of the harvest

Will pluck your soul

Evermore

Ruins of the Titans Part 1

by FD Ravenskraft

Darkest days as the light stare
In a glare coming from the sky
Of musty decayed bodies
As it is raining blood
And screaming of innocence men, women, and children
Are three-course meals being digested in horror
We all are doom
By the inside of their bellies
Within the ruins of the giants
In the midst, there continues
Being eating and swallow you whole
The abyss of the stomach
You will disorder
You will rest a shame
Within the asylum of solitude
Lies within the piles of bodies
As they rise
They're out the blood in the darkest hour
The giants of cannibalism
As they eat each other
It the fashion of devouring humans
Are itching for revenge for their ancestor's lives
The squad coming and guards are reading
Kill the titan
Slaughter the Gods
Of a horizon for time

She Plays Her Violin Concerto (The End of Beauty)

by FD Ravenskraft

She plays the tune of the ages

To calm the winds. And the passion of the mare's forbidden sins

Making love to the string of the violin

Like a whore comes before Jezebel's galore

She opens the seals of the box of Pandora

To destroy all thing on the oral of that order

The winds are in rage

And the oceans are composing

The screaming of the dutchman's crew

The songs of decomposing as the dead that drowns here

Is singing the choral fantasy of pure madness

As she plays in the form of darkly beautiful

Harvest her sound. As she caresses the hellhounds

As they are howling the psalms that the devil spoke

And the heavens close their ears

Because of the horror sound of pure beauty

The winds are in tears

And the oceans are collecting the tears of the angels.

She raised the dead with her Merlin's soul

And played and played

In till the Gods was hypnotized and she causes them to have an orgy

Of the century

A Ragnarök festival

The thunderstorms are the pure sounds she needs

The lightning struck down

As she lusts for the power of the sirens

As they give harmony with her touch

And the anger of the demons devour each other

The passion for the annihilation

To return the horror of recreation

Foolish girl

Your sound is so beautiful

But your playing is killing us all

She plays and playing in till she stops

Her violin concerto

Has end and everything around her

Is nothing there but a flooded civilization

On top of a huge rock

Is her and she ages into an old hag

No longer she can play

She's fading away and her skin is flaking

Time come for her

And death embrace

There's nothing there but her violin

Playing in her ghostly form

The end of it all

The Narrator

The Madness of The Undertaker

by FD Ravenskraft

The midst of the madness of purity
And the darkness is my savior
Coming forth furthermore
Nothing more that a seed of a whore
So soon I unseen the seen horror
Of all
We been more than that
That the game has started for the killing of all
I compose this warning of the unseen terror
Alas. The Foolishness of the woe
The emptyiness of the soul
Buried alive in the Evening of the dem of hallows
I see myself
But not thyself
An immortal my beloved
Dead and decay
Making love to her corpse
Knowing I will die and hope to lay with her
Forever rotten
Forever coming
No longer want too.
But to undertake myself
The Narrator

Paint It Black

by FD Ravenskraft

For the Verses of Terror

The darkness blends in the mind of the consciousness.

The blackness of the crimes of my rhyme.

The bliss of the fatal kiss.

But you wish. You never become this.

As humanity is my puppets

To tear them into submission.

The beauty of torture

The blackest of my soul.

Never mind I'm bored in this lonesome cold.

Freezing by the heart

Mutilated their skin with a branding iron

Just to enjoy the screaming.

Destroy them like the monster they are,

But by far. I'm the tortured czar

Burying my victims in my backyard

for most I impaled them, just to be seen.

On top of the world.

Knowing I have a place in hell.

I covered their bodies in honey.

Just for the maggot and gnats to slowly devour the corpse,

I'm being this cursive dick.

That enjoying the torture to play with their souls.

I painted everything black.

As my eyes drown in blood

The lettering of their agony.

As the sack is full of torso snacks.

As the emptiness of life.

That caress thee

Into the delightful knight

Within the night of deadly fright.

In the skies.

The ravens rely to feast on scraps of the broken

I have spoken in tongues

Before I was awoken with my own song

The leftovers I had for them.

As my victims continue screaming.

Flaying their skin with the blade.

Slicing slowly before me

I see nothing but trash. That rape the souls of

The innocence.

There's no justice

But mine.

They will repay for their lies

The dead speak my name.

Within the shame of brutal games.

No one will claim you

But I'm your host.

Whips and chains

Nooses and Pendulums

Will be forever your home

Bastards of reality.

You never escape me

Believe you will see.

End

The Narrator

We're the Lonesome fog

by FD Ravenskraft

For the Verses of Terror
In the midst of the fogs
We all see the spirits within it
By the docks buried by the logs
Are the madness of angry Wraiths
Trapped like a fish being drawn to the bait
Only to be catch. But for them not so well
In hell they being devour and dispose of
Like a decay soiled doves
That can't no longer fly
But died in the heat where they lie
But the mist speak to us
Like the smog of London
They speak in tongues
In they haunted beautiful song
When it comes for the fog to dismissed
They're still here unseen
Only at night they scream the songs of dream
No longer their souls redeem
Just to wait to the mist return
For they're story to be finished
The Narrator

The Sonnets of a Madman

by FD Ravenskraft

For the Verses of Terror
The brutality of the self-depraved mind
They composed a sense of breed that bleeds out the sounds.
Of the corrupted. The madness of it all that has a crown.
The unseen being feeding off the souls and puking out.
The leftovers of insanity. The darkness aware of the unfair horror
That is scope like a sea of untamed dreams.
At the beginning of it all. The curse of the mind
Is spoiled by depression and control for the sake of reality.
To see yourself repeat in the state of death.
The blackness of a Man's heart is like a dark forest.
Quiet and deranged. The endangered species of all mankind
Poisoning us all
The cleansing of the cold-hearted being.
Noticing the scopes of nightmares
Broken and slowly healing. The sonnets of madness
The symphony of life and the encore
Of digging your own grave
This is my insanity. That doesn't make sense to me.
By writing this. Blinded by cruelty and abuse.
I'm composing the horror of them all.
To only die in the fountain of age
A dark reincarnation of a Poet.
An author of his own demise
No more corrupted lies.
I end this in stanzas of Volumes
The Narrator

The Lodgers of the Fog

by FD Ravenskraft

The silent of the great one
The song of the smog spreading smoke
Into the city. As London breathes
And the clutches of the Fog
A night like any night
Murderous midnight
No more than a fright as they say
Every corner is a body lying on cold street
Between the lodge of Whitechapel and Slade street
This is not another Ripper story
But others as well. Beside ol dear jack
The Golem of Limehouse
And others in between
What else the great mother's hiding in her isles
In the crowded streets of unsung dreams
Murder ink written with a blade
But the fog hidden secrets
Of lifeless bodies under the bridge still stands
Forgive me it wont fall down
Thy fair lady closed the deal
Even after Jack done and gone. The legends
Is still blends
And dank.
Knowingly the fog tells familiar tales
Of mayhem
With a shank. The tales of the Lodgers
Will haunt the history within the minds
Of the living.
The smog compose the screams of the unworthy
The presence of the Dead
I end this in Volumes

The Narrative Monster

by FD Ravenskraft

For The Verse of Terror

Ladies and Gentlemen

Welcome to my rhyme

I shall tell you a tale

And you don't have to spend a dime

But only your life. Is worth more

Allow me to open the door

Into a world of nothing more

Than pure horror and Mayhem

No escape my beautiful adore

A word from our sponsor

To sell your soul to me. The monster

And collect your thoughts

And hypnotize your mind

To drain every ounce of your being

Welcome back to the show

You forgotten about me through

But I haven't miss you at all

Just waiting for you to tune in to continue

The story that will unfold

The tall tale heartless glow

The tale has ended

Yes I'm honored to Narrated

And give and take.

Till next time I tell you a tale

Coming from the gates of hell

Till next time

Goodnight

The Twilight Of The Writers

by FD Ravenskraft

Based on The Twilight of the Gods

I see them in the clouds

Composing their last song

The writers of the dawn

We are Poets our will be done

Unfolding and unsung

We're the Gods of the Twilight

Writing in the names of the Holy

Our tongue speaks for itself

For it worth. We're The Gods of Wordsmithing

The Skalds of this century

Born from the tongue of the Viking soul

The time has begun

For our ghostly compose tongue

Our words are swift and bold

Our stories never untold

Our breastplate are the souls of the Pen

Never forget our rhyme begins

The House of The Watchtower

by FD Ravenskraft

As the light beams in song
Preparing the aftermath of dawn
The house is compose a symphonic score
As the night the Raven's will scorn
All along the watchtower
The lighthouse of dimmed
As the oceanside breaths the chanting
Crows. Woe. The Sweetest one
adore the light is done
To the next one will tell a story
To end all glory

The Imaginary Murders

by FD Ravenskraft

In the curse of the night. as the creatures of havoc unite

We're the killers of the fields of dreamy delight

Come forth fools of the improper scene of broken dreams

As you all scream from this unseen. seen

Monsters of imaginary horror scenes. where all things die

And the hope of a dying cursive lie

A beautiful and creative double homicide

It seems to me that

The lust of the blade. is floating your way as you sleep

In the bed of roses that is your wet red wine

Would you like to play with me?

I take you to the other side as the fallen bodies emerge

And piled up like swapmeet. as the beauty of it all

The tender of the invincible kill

Wakes up child hears your folks. never mind who dreams

The mark of this town. even the Gods are afraid of the murderous crown

The coming three of the dark master

Roams to control the murders of your friends

You imagine so well. I come to you with this tale

From the page of the Dis of hell

The dead will speak of these despicable wraiths

As the victims of the unknown breed of imaginary seeds

They're still here as the ghostly creed

To end all and feed

Remember bastards of the young

They kill you with a kiss

As you're being dismiss

From the masters of the abyss

Woe Woe

In the name by the door.

The mother of the unseen whore

Taking revenge by the command of the three

The seen of unholy bliss

Remember were here

Tis Tis

You're will not be missed

Gladly

The Antichrist Horrors

by FD Ravenskraft

The demise of the valley

The sickness of the rivers

Seas and oceans decayed with bodies of old

The madness of humanity

Killings and the purges

The clouds blacken and the sun is red blood

Cannibals eating each other

Branded and numb

The animals are now grasping for food

But eating the leftover of the dead

Stinking and forbidden

The governments of our lands

Having oral orgy just to past the time

As the party goes on

As the rest of the world is dying of starvation

Myself is watching in horror

Impaled by spikes as they feed off my

Liquid

I tear the last drop

As the rapid dogs feed off me

I'm the antichrist that will give you heaven

I'm the antichrist that will serve hell on a plate

But instead,

You displeased me

With your greed

You feed off me like I'm moist and delight

Your Christ will come

I'm the new Rome

The Caesar of your nightmares

My bosom is Cleopatra's bowels

Now feed all you want

You only destroying yourself

This is your Holocaust

I'm will be your extinction

Your Christ will save you

The devil will feed off your leftover

I'm the Antichrist superstar

Now

The Moriarty Boxcar Slaughter Machine

by FD Ravenskraft

The dark skies spell his name

Caught by threads of his victims

The cruel. The brave and the suits of authority

Enter the train of the Red Moriarty

Feed of the blood of the injustice

The ones that commit the terror

Of citizens

The innocence that was abuse the law of the lands

Now vengeance has it's name

Pigs. Suits. Military slugs

Porky swine disgrace by they oath

Must taste the train's fury

The demonic stream trains

Rides the track in hell's wheels

The corpse are use for oil and blood screams intercourse

Within the bloody belly of the train core

Moriarty

Moriarty

Red adore

Eat them

Smoke them

Ride on by

Trail along and eat the livestock

Of the law

Suck up their souls

When they perish

Their stock is yours

Pleasure grave

Ride on the trails of hell

The Horror of Sonnets

by FD Ravenskraft

Lock in the chamber of bars

So unbelievable and extremely hard

Lost but no found in the psych ward of life

The madness continue to blend

Broken in the crumbles of sin

In the house of the creature's den

Of the upbringing of revenge

The bitterness of the night

Lock in the cage of raging rodents

The Mares of night collecting the feces

To create another form of me

Being crucified for being the dark one

Never found but lost in distress

Wanting to caress in my own empty nest

But being in a fatal test

To out beat the best

In the breastplate of insanity

Being marked in the strait jacket vest

But in front of me are the ghost of my dark pass

Walking on green grass of the dead

That's not much to say

That my sanity is delayed

Coming forth to depend on the gang of strays

As I'm lying down speaking in tongues

To finally sing the compose unsung

The Slothful Meeting

by FD Ravenskraft

The fools are coming

And the year of the sloths is the harvest of its kin

But the food was placed here

And the sins of their fathers

Has commit adultery

The meeting is now in session

They sit and have intercourse

And feast on their greed

And manipulate in vicious pride

The envious have fallen into their purge

But they feel that the lust of kings must give them.

What they must desire

The sins of their ministry

The dissimulation of fools

The relation of many chapters

In the books of the fall of Eden

Many Adams

More creeds of Eve

And the devil of thousands

In the meeting of sloths

Their singing in the pile of groups

Laying together with God

Took away their access

In starvation

The harvest of cannibals

They light up the candles

Alive and well

As they sacrifice themselves

And start eating each other

Screaming in pain

So severe.

That their devouring the flesh and collecting the torso for

Dessert,

The deadly sins are watching this event

According to the records

Hell has entered the meeting

And the devil has the final say as he finishes the last of the leftovers

Only to spit them out to devour again

In the bowels of the beast

The harvest is done

The Diary of the Plague Doctor's Score

by FD Ravenskraft

The pendulum strikes the lands
With the sickness of disease
Coming forth the rage of the summit demise
In my diary, I compose the scene of the divided
Being if Death's Galore in the cold
Of a dying breed and the bodies are sold to the highest bidder
In the Mass graves of the unblessed
The beginning in my composed masterpiece
I see the dying like an unwritten index of a page
Curse like a stray in heat
Decomposed in a fashion of bitterness

You'll face the Madness within
As we will bend down the sounds of scream
The chambers of piled graves
I see the laughter of death
Trying to save them all. His abyss is strong
Like the levees of contaminated oceans
The garden of soil are filthy and grim
My paper is my bloodletting

Midnight dreary in the series of that year
The terror we all feared the bubonic symphony
On the year of 47. Curse of 13 AD
We all will die and remember this day
I write my last
Dying and buried in the Mass
Keep my symphonies
To remember thee
No longer I shall see
Breathless without a plea

Fin
The Narrator

The Flowers of Evil

by FD Ravenskraft

Hush hush

Quiet in the closet

Don't scream i will ease your pain

I need red paint to create my art

The passion i have to make my creativity

My murderous masterpiece

Come on dear love me softly

Trust me it doesn't bother me

Caress my hands with your bloody Grasps

I find your heart warming

To consider this task

Looking through the mirror

Of the undying glass

I see you

You see me

I am the final plea

It wouldn't end well

I promise you will see

Hush hush

My little sissy

Now you wish you miss me

I send you flowers

After I end you with pure evil

The Talltale Reaper

by FD Ravenskraft

I feel it coming

A talltale is written

It's the harvest of the reaper

Three knocks at the door

Silence

Again three knocks

Silence

No noise to be exact

The door open

And a book was in front of the door

I pick it up

Shivering with fear

I open the book

No words exist within this talltale

But was grab and force in the book of death

To serve him

Eternal

Leave Me In The Cold

by FD Ravenskraft

For the Verses of Terror

Left me in the room to be torture

Mindlessly within the Madness of time.

You say your useless for someone like me.

In my dark world i belong.

Lock me up in the temptation of a cold life.

My love the insanity you bring to my unforgiven heart.

Dying in the cold where I lay

My weary head. The dreary of it all

The fall of the intense. Upon the darkness

Caressing the mayhem of her love.

The coolness being buried alive.

Scared and afraid. Freezing in the motion

Of no escape.

Leave me in the cold.

Leave thee in the cold.

My love you're bold.

Living by the Women's code.

You left me to die.

But now I dive into the lower plains

Why death come to me

Darkness is my true lover

My pen is my Narration

Forgive me I'm a fool

Death is my ally

The madness of it all

She poison thee

With her poisonous tongue

Now I sleep

The Psycho's Garden

by FD Ravenskraft

The harvest has come
And the end of the body counts has begun
Let freedom ring and your welcome will come to a Terrible end
Within the Garden of Psycho lurks to collect his feed
The souls of the damned
The corruption of mankind
Are looking for him
The angels and demons
The cutting psycho
The Garden is infected
The first stage of insanity
comes with a price
He's eating the souls of the wicked
The Garden of Stone stains blood
It sheds it because of the voice of a God
That bleeds out the word mother of all
Summoning out the paragram of the devil's symbol
It's cold and dank
His unholy will
Devours the flesh of the dead
And sniff the dust like a drug addicted
Fresh bodies are collected for ritual
as he bathes in decay to nourish his skin
The more he collects the deeper the spiral
The Garden is sad
But enjoying the vacancy
raping the souls
The Garden is never full
You useless tool he's the reason for your doom
The stones will collect the soil
The garden will collect
The Psycho will show some respect
Regardless

The Tinker Tinker Crackling Kraken

by FD Ravenskraft

Trinket trinket little
There's the kraken
Floating like a corrupted star
With his tentacles
Within the skies he flows and flows
To find himself in destiny's grasp
The machine eats and more
To drink the evil of spoiled souls
To corrupted the nations
The machine that floats to eat the balance
Of the sins of man.
The alien cannibal
Tin machine in all
Eats and eats it's little things.
Now the world's end
Has it's end
The cracking laugh
Tinker trinket
Little blood the kraken
Trinket is not a star
The falling doom
Waiting for his feast
Of human swine
Nothing more
Nothing less
The screaming laugh
Is your death galore
Trinket trinket
Tittle star.
There's the kraken
Chaos for all

The Dirty Orchestra

by FD Ravenskraft

The crowd is stun to see the madness within the players

Of gnostic feel

The musicians having incest with passionate appeal

The compilation of a sexual delight

The conductor is pleased to see his creation in motion

The forbidden love-making with each other

Their ripping off their clothes having pure intercourse

As the dirty babylon continues to broil as the crowd

Sees the sexual fortissimo

The adagio of the F major

The menace of all pride

Straight lace even gays with all means

The lesbian method and all sex having

A pathetique sence of melody with their bodies

The maestro join in within the night

All the crowd is having the De' sade favor

And all together the sex fest is more heated

All together now the maestro says

All genres of different styles of sex join in

The allegro of dirty deeds

The night of the symphony was the opera

Of intercourse

And it ended with a plague

Croatoan has come

To claim his victim

The encore of the last symphony

Ends in sexual bliss

The Skeleton's Crush

by FD Ravenskraft

He watches her from far away

No longer has his flesh

Not even a heart

But he feels her love within

His emptiness

As his bones wants to make love to her

As his soul trapped

Because of her

He needs to be caressed

And she knows it's her lover

That perish so long ago

She mourns for him

For so long

That they might meet

Once again

She kissed him

As they both

Promise each other forever

But cannot touch

She will wait for him

But for now

The bone king will see her safety

In his arms only

The Sonnets of a Madman

by FD Ravenskraft

The brutality of the self-coincidence mind

The compose sense of breed that bleeds out the sounds.

Of the corrupted. The madness of it all that it has a crown.

The unseen being feeding of the souls and puking out.

The leftovers of insanity.

The darkness aware of the unfair horror

That is scope like a sea of untamed dreams.

In the beginning of it all.

The curse of the mind

Is spoiled by depression and control by the sake of reality.

To see yourself repeat in the state of death.

The blackness of a Man's heart is like a dark forest.

Quiet and deranged.

The endangered species of all mankind

Poisoning us all

The cleansing of the cold-hearted being.

Noticing the scopes of nightmares

Broken and slowly healing.

The sonnets of madness

The symphony of life and the encore

Of digging your own grave

This is my insanity. That don't make sense to me.

By writing this. Blinded by cruelty and abuse.

I'm composing the horror of them all.

To only die in the fountain of age

A dark reincarnation of a Poet.

An author of his own demise

No more corrupted lies.

I end this in stanzas of Volumes

The Literature Murder Show

by FD Ravenskraft

In the room full of people
It is an event where the invitation.
Is your last
Within the theatre
The author reads and everyone listens.
To the words of the wise as they obey
Did not realize their time has come.
With no delay
Refreshment in the lobby
Filled with poison and arsenic blend is his hobby.
Drinking yourself to death for a tasty
Beverage ice cold
Obey your thirst.
Of this murderous curse
The author continues reading.
Realizing everyone is going to die.
He smiles with a grin.
Caressing his literature sin
To find them all dead
By his passionate Dredd
A marvelous slain
An endless slowly pain
Bodies fall.
Inside the theatre
He eats them all.
And swallows them whole.
Sessions over
The Narrator

The Kiss of Death's Grasp

by FD Ravenskraft

He seeks to be loved.

But more he lost his special glove.

That she gave him.

He buried her in his realm.

To only find an empty tomb.

Till he realizes the moment of truth

Repeatedly.

He inhales every ounce of her being.

Boneless and skull.

What is left.

Only him and a tomb of nothing.

What he grasps.

Was an empty soul.

The Narrator

Dark Roast

by FD Ravenskraft

Fine coffee. fresh coffee

Sugar so sweet

Dark roast grains

The taste of death remains.

The rhymes so clear and spoke.

A coffee shop right down the English's shore

Where people drink coffee and java everyday

To find peace and taste

Where poets and writers are delighted to know

Each other

The spoken word on Sunday evening

But the old and odd times

How some people

Wonder the customer disappear!

For period

The cops of Scotland yard

Wonder around the shop and notice

A strong smell of corpse near by the cellar

They went down basement to find bodies of all.

Of all poets and writers

And ghostwriter

Slumbered on top of each other.

10 to 20 bodies.

Must been poison inside them.

The investigation to piece together

This place is the catacomb.

These murders took a toll.

Fine coffee. Fresh coffee

Sugar so sweet

Dark roast grain

The taste of deaths remains.

The rhymes so clear and solid

The police saw this as the sociopath.

Work of art

Arsenic powder and

Blood's delight

For a month, the search for him not

With a cup of coffee and writers too

Right down the other side of London

Besides the tower

They write and drink.

Enjoying your brew of caffeine

And java

Welcome everyone and enjoy!

The smooth taste and the smell of it

O willingly Poet

Have a cup of Joe.

No no you have been warn.

The Mincemeat Society.
(The Cannibal's Paradise)

by FD Ravenskraft

My taste is sizzling.

For fresh meat. a deluxe favor I admire and a rich texture of the upper torso.

To marinade the skin with delicious sauce

Come to our table and allow us to feast in your harvest.

In your honor

Bon appetit your skin deep.

Past the mustard

The prophecy of the end of humanity.

As the bodies of the dead lay in front of me.

And it seems beautiful of demise you see.

There is no plea. But a final scene.

Of this endless forbidden dream

Coming for me in his bold manner

As he sale his soul. As he becomes fatter

The meat of his choice is human deluxe.

Do not make a fust as this man it curses.

Human meat is being grind into perfection.

For it to blend the favor

The sizzling of the skin. Lingering the texture

The mincemeat so tasty and lusting.

The garden of human flesh is being collected.

For the feast of the Gods

Eating away why they are alive.

As the endure tortured marinade

The knife and folk pierce the skin

The endless scream. So intense

And demanding none

The hunger of the club

Has come to it last meal.

Then the commander demands

An orgy. but instead, their eating each other

In a sexual symphony

The fantastic remedy of devouring obsession of hunger

To the last man

The table of twelve is dead.

Eating to death and the one

Will collect their bodies.

To dispose of them for the harvest

In till the next orgy

The Whispers of Torture

by FD Ravenskraft

You are a beast reincarnated.

And he is the victim of your rage.

And no one seems to bear.

Or nothingness of a caring souls

When pain crosses the mind of the weak.

I compose their relief

From the miserable grief.

Allow me to prove to those I can heal you

With thy method of madness.

I whisper in your ear.

To tell you I will serve

And take upon myself to remove your pain.

And wrongdoing I will correct.

I have a secret

And a graveyard as necessary,

you know longer must endure

Your vengeance I will serve you

Foolish men and all that seek harm

Allow me to compose my symphony

You are being tied to the chair

Now you are in my crosshair

Being in the fashion of torture

You cannot escape the hell I bring you

Lock in the cage being fed scraps from your

From own feces. As the rest being burn alive

As my kin watches and learn my methods

Can you escape the midst of my rage?

You will never leave in till I say

In the cage where no can find you.

When I done
You no longer function your life
The same.
Everywhere I go
I see others in pain
I hide and endure their suffering
But not for long
When I see you in agony?
And protecting is scorn
What the pigs will not do
I shall have to pleasure
To accept and carry your burden
And brutality enjoy
The screams of the culprits
They will not bother you
As my darkness shall guild me
Into the depth of no return
I will enjoy
Craving their souls alive
Flaying my victims
In the religion of abuse
Tasty you think.

The Mechanical Succubus

by FD Ravenskraft

The world built a machine
Beyond the days of old
Before the first flood of noah
A rage against the humanity
The sins of two noble lovers
Their sins to find immortality
Their greed of fierce of needing
Bliss of naughty and nice
They want their own babylon and found
Their answer. Within the valley of bathsheba
Where gate shape with the image of a mechanical
succubus hiding behind it the tree of life
Is their answer to bring their lusting deed
The nightmare hour
The lands darken
Their enter towards the gate to The key
Nothing there to open
But it secrets unknown
To find their answer
Their read the riddles by the gateway
With these words clear as day. only
Incest open the cradle within the beast.
Crown.
They made love in steaming heat
In order to rule their dreams of sodomy
Their semen open the succubus gate
In order to find the tree decay in darken

Bliss. The hidden beast suck them in draining their life

And gate close only for machine

To attack the world

Sucking the air out

Of the earth for the sins of the lovers

To create the wasteland of all lands

Now their sins is in the belly of

Lilith's seed

The dusk of humanity is their graves of the Saharan catacombs

End

The Brain Feast

by FD Ravenskraft

The apocalypse has arrived

And the human's food chain is now a new dish

A taste treat that will change the world for the worst

A forbidden tale of ruthless curse

The plague feast of eating brain of genius

And madmen

The insane asylum is now packed with cannibal corpses

Yes indeed the fatal end of course

People eating each other

For the taste of brains

Black noon cross the lands

Rapid dogs killing like the harvest dance

Devouring the nature of men

The feast now begun and everyone

Is dying

No rest for the wicked crying as it seem

Sickness scorns the badlands

And the waste

Come with me my children

Of the numb

Let us die and make haste

And eat within the blood of sin

Within the catching fire

Hell on earth is now televised

The children will eat the leftover

We will prevail

Silence of the Goats

by FD Ravenskraft

The goats have escaped
The asylum of limbo
I'm there to investigate their Sins
To find out about their murderous ways
The killings of Angels
And their cannibalism of demons
Looking for them
Following the endless bodies
Of humans
Corrupted and cruel

I am a poet composing in hell
Under Satan
An informant for God
A tally to tell the heart
Without reason

The war of the Goats
Their murderous silence
They want me
Dead…
I dream this endless death
That God feeds me to the Goats

Ha ha Satan replies
You're mine...
Forever I'm yours
Father of hell

The Chicken Man

by FD Ravenskraft

The prince of the dark arts

You make a deal and break it

You will drown in the dock

Of the Georgia slum

For your crimes against the grain

Drowning in bloody rain

If you need a favor call upon the Chicken Man

But cross him and you will see his fury

Tied and bondage for his chickens to feast on your soul

The craving of the Rooster

As it crows three times that when you know

Your time has come for him to take his prize

Upon the house of the rising sun

The chicken man will fillet you and cook you done

After he kill you for betraying his bond

Never make a deal

With the Chick. Chick. Chick

Chicken Man

His will shall be done

Death Fair Massacre

by FD Ravenskraft

The midst of decayed Melody
In the tall tales of a affair of thee
Drinking the blood
Of the mutilated few
Set aside the gruesome new
Bodies everywhere
Blood and guts in the hands of the cannibal
Yes we are animals
Within the kingdom of slaughter
Nothing more of course don't bother
To save anymore
My bowels are full
I eat the world
The Massacre tells a story
And ends with a fatal encore
This is the nameless tragedy
A death affair
With a common stare
A intake of a brutal ink
The beginning of a endless end
The plague finally won
The death toll
Everyone
Mass graves are our resting place
Our doom is our requirements
A requiem in hell

Ring Around The Corpses

by FD Ravenskraft

The children sing the horror

Nursery rhyme lore...

Preparing to eat the corpse

In Hansel's pot where Gretel built

The children sing as the bodies escaped

The potty gold of steaming broiled hell

Ring around the corpses

Pocket full of fingers

Ashes. Ashes. We all get cook

As they sing the pot overflow

They try to escape

As limbo's burning furnace

Increases its temperature

The scream known they about to be eaten

By the corn children

They are done now

The feast

Is soon

The song

The rhyme

Is done

Inker of The Dawned

by FD Ravenskraft

My pen is the plague

The ink consumes me

My hands are vexed

And my mind relax and flow

The evil within

The monsters in my head tell me

What to say

I create the world in my own image

For only for reality to shatter

To piece

Everyone dies in their sleep

And eating by the fiends of

Midsummer's creep

I notice my mind is damage

I'm going insane

Come to life my demons

Feast upon the damned

Everyone shall be harvest

They're no prayers for me

I have dawned the world with my ink

Drowned them from the brink of their own

Insanity

Even by the hands of me

I drive myself till oblivion

The Turn of The Blade

by FD Ravenskraft

The cut within the slice
Perfection as it craves the skin
Caressing the knife
As the blade
Grasps the feeling of a deepthroat
End
You can feel the torture
As the blade drills the blood out
As thicken
Deeper you drill
The spilling of red oil
Collects the muscles
As you scream bloody murder
Before you know it
The top hat jack
Is ripping you silently
The ripper is calling
Obey and die within
The midst
Of his intense
Unconditional love affair
His blade

Sin

by FD Ravenskraft

He lusted for her as she submitted

Her romantic grasp to teach him

The ropes of discipline for her special event

The madame is ready for her cookies to be baked

Nice and moist for her men

You just walked into the lion's den

Because you definitely commit a sin

The whip that the beholder seize

To control and make her deviants obey her

As he is tied in naughty bondage

Please submit to her now

Address her and bow

To her forbidden sin

The training has begun

The teacher shall have its pet

The night will be scorn within the Domme's pit

Love is rough

But not such love exists

Just naughty fun

Tis Tis

The Coach of The Sadist Horsemen

by FD Ravenskraft

The Horsemen is riding hard with his iron whip
With his coach shallow dreams...
Nothing more but his blood drips
Slowly as he is needing a lover to bathed him
But instead his sadist soul deceive his urge
His red eyes hypnotize his victim for naughty pleasure
To his castle de krafts
For him to command his dirty deeds
The asylum of intercourse is his domain
To love to bear
And ease even despair
His lover tickle his shaggy hair
To caress his needs to share his adoring dare
Once upon the midsummer's nights
The rooms are full the invitation is done
For the night of the flocks.
Bondage season
Sadist's greetings
Dominate obedience
Moaning glory
Sizzling spice compose it's naughty and nice
The Commander respects his peers
As the party must go on
The Harvest is calling more soiled delicious banshees
For his pleasure to succeed his expectation
In till morning when the horsemen rides
And his coach swallows his victims
Some are dead and the rest parties on
Because the cry of the dark horse
Is inevitable
He will see you again in the next dead season
His whip will rule again

The Harvest of the Tainted Ones

by FD Ravenskraft

Within the harvest

The hunger of the ghouls

As humanity are the targets for the food chain

It has come to the reign of the sins of bloody rain

For a reason of this madness

The cause of this disease

Is the greed of dirty little sins

Of seven corrupted parasites of man,

The sight of the hellish dogs

That can use their might

To try and fight God's holy might

On that day when the earth has died

And the humans push aside to be fresh meat

Within the belly of Solomon

I seek the refuge for a one last of freedom

To only find myself being chewed and spit out over again

By the Tainted Ones

The ghouls will have their day when the last of humanity is gone

They will eat other

Just to keep the food chain

As it rains.

The levee of bodies will surface

My mass grave will be my last

Horrorcore

by FD Ravenskraft

I'm the villain in red

Compose his flows from within and before the dead

I see myself in moral dredd

Trying to find closure within myself

As I'm choking you to death

You know the color the villain in red

I'm dying over and over again

Every time myself is suffering the horror begins

Unclear that I am a burden

For those who seek me

Do you understand or are you certain

I'm the core of pure horror

The realist of the real

A poet in rage

To show the world

I have turn the next chapter of the page

Come to me and seek the truth

Of my own horrorcore

Once Upon A Midnight Dreary

by FD Ravenskraft

Upon the madness accrue

A poet's sin never far from the pour of

A demon's grin to compose the light

That darkness eating fright

Once no time at all

Within the tall tale sins of the fall

Season as the leaves blacken the deadly reason

Of the dreary call

My symphony of Lenore

The pendulum of the tortured shore

No matter what

My sweet adore

I'm the creeper of midnight

The fright of an Abyssinians light

Once upon the twilight's dawn

In the seas of unpleasant dreams

In the cursive world of unclean and filthy

As my pen bleeds red

Draining my victims

The last supper of our daily bread

Bloody hell

The devil expelled

As Baltimore bleeds the name

Everyone knows the same

Darken bliss is Edgar's gain

The cat is watching me from beyond my insanity

I have nothing left but my pen in front of me

And the candlelit up as I compose my time

To write the blasphemous work

The forbidden crime

I shall die in the wasteland

In the open graves of desserts

To be eating and prey by the lust of blizzards

The soil is grave

Nothing more

None delayed

The Chamber of Doors

by FD Ravenskraft

Within the chambers

Of the forbidden doors

Comes the age it murderous galore

In the twisted fate of chaos

Within the doors of the mind

The plague of a tortured soul

The feeling of the dark matter within the mind

Of his tormentor

Many doors have the chamber lock

The forbidden place to go

Open one the pandora's box

Within the world of many

As the dark garden blossom in the decay of the stray of madness

Connecting the dots of insanity

Caress the remedy of nightmares

The straightforward of many places

Within the mind coming

Intact to find yourself in the state

Of mystery beyond the measures

Of being trapped

The saga continues

The Skeleton's Crush

by FD Ravenskraft

He watches her from far away

No longer has his flesh

Not even a heart

But he feels her love within

His emptiness

As his bones wants to make love to her

As his soul trapped

Because of her

He needs to be caressed

And she knows it's her lover

That perish so long ago

She mourns for him

For so long

That they might meet

Once again

She kissed him

As they both

Promise each other forever

But cannot touch

She will wait for him

But for now

The bone king will see her safety

In his arms only

The Wrath Of The Rose For The Omen

by FD Ravenskraft

The ignorance of the sin

Blessed is the blissful grin

Nothing more

Hiding behind the rose of war

Received by anger

The violent blessing

Caress the soul

As the red flood

Compose the Symphony of Rage

To begin to turn the next Page

The Lust of the Roses for HIMM

By FD Ravenskraft

The Dead breaths into a shattered dream

Lying in decay as it seems

The Lust of the Lonesome Rose

That caress the story that is told

Into bliss of the Florist

The Storyteller untold

That folds the cycle of the

Bachelor as his lover's seen

The end of it all

The blood flows into the rose

To tell a tale about

The lust of Hell

This is the first sin

More will come

On the darker Eve

The message will be deceived

The Twilight of The Writers

by FD Ravenskraft

Based on The Twilight of the Gods

I see them in the clouds

Composing their last song

The writers of the dawn

We are Poet. we will be done

Unfolding and unsung

We're the Gods of the Twilight

Writing in the names of the Holy

Our tongue speaks for itself

For it worth. We're The Gods of Wordsmithing

The Skalds of this century

Born from the tongue of the Viking soul

The time has begun

For our ghostly compose tongue

Our words are swift and bold

Our stories are never untold

Our breastplates are the souls of the Pen

Never forget our rhyme begins

The Intercourse Ball

by FD Ravenskraft

The beast has arrived

Because his last victims all died

He collects the mysteries of their souls

Devours them

And consume

Constantly composing their eternal doom

The torso feast for the cunning beast

Every slut participates

In the intercourse dinner

The ball of the sinners

Waltz of the harvest

Garden of bodies being nourish

To be fertilize

And mutilated

As the heart and lung being wrapped to be mummified

And roasted to perfection

A sacrificial table manner

Ripping the skin as the life meal

Screams in pure horror

This a fantasy of a choral

As they sing and drink to honor

The whore goddess

Of Babylon

Tis without a season

In the belly of the Gods

We all shall plea

Because at the end

We all delete

The Mourning of the Tune of her Tears for HIMM

by FD Ravenskraft

The Tune that curses the Polaris Skies.

Everything so weary and completely died.

In the Rivers where the Dead lies.

In the bed of the mating of Flies.

She plays the Opus of a Dark Cries.

Within the Mourning Passion Play

Her Symphony never dies.

The Quarantine of the lost.

She's the Queen of all cost.

The Beauty of the Holocaust

Her adagio is a poetic tune.

The ruin of humanity is their doom.

The Violin compose the enchanting gloom

As the Gregorian spit the harmony of all

As she plays

All the legends shall fall

She is my Pathetique

My beautiful mystique

I pray the lord my soul shall not keep

Only to weep in the Abyss

And drown in her tears of loneliness of the deep

Jack's Mortem

by FD Ravenskraft

A women's nightmare
Is the ugly brutal stare
As he operation on the floors
Of Whitechapel
As he left his victims
To rot on the grounds of old England
His motivation
Is his intense notification
To murder every slut as possible
Knowing in his wrong
But don't care
The Mortem of the man of coldness
As he is bold
In the city of weakness
As he can't be caught
As he multiplate
Method curses the British Isle
Jack the lad
The streets of the sad
His legendary
Is settle in hell
White chapel and Slade Street
Would be hunted by his thirst
He is the monster
The bowel of the beast
The common murderer
His old Bailey
Is the eternal noose
Of The devil's hand
England's monster
Would forever burn
In the Twilight of the Pit

The Lust of The Roses or HIMM

by FD Ravenskraft

The Dead breaths into a shattered dream

Lying in decay as it seems

The Lust of the Lonesome Rose

That caress the story that is told

Into bliss of the Florist

The Storyteller untold

That folds the cycle of the

Bachelor as his lover's seen

The end of it all

The blood flows into the rose

To tell a tale about

The lust of Hell

This is the first sin

More will come

On the darker Eve

The message will be deceived

The Rose of the Stone Garden for HIMM Horror

by FD Ravenskraft

The darker abyss for the lusting part

As the heart falls into an upstart

The bleeding of the deceased lover that whole

A rose he picks from his decayed bones

Like a song of the fallen

Blessed as the dark harvest calling

For her. but he waits in agony

As she touches and loves another

With this broken heart his red rose

Becomes the new heart

And know he realizes there's no turning back

In the land of the Delightful

The dead has a place for him

His new lover is the gardens of stones

The Verses of Terror Presents: A Beautiful Night

by FD Ravenskraft

The Mares of Whores

Knocking on my chamber door

Free from to roam the Twilight

Of the forbidden midnight

A beautiful night to kill

A night of thrills

The flight of the demons

As the banshees scream in a symphony of fright

The Wolves Howl

Hungry for meat

The dead poets celebrate

The coming of the Night God

As the poetess eat their rotten flesh

Thy will be done says him

A beautiful night to devour

The grace of Christ

The last supper of the deceased

Oh Come thy thee faithful

To deny the truth of the corrupted light

We will prevail

The Wraiths

The banshees

And all things roam the night

We are one

Thou will be done

The Narrator

The Goats of The Rodeo

by FD Ravenskraft for The Verses of Terror

The hounds of hell
Escaped the bowels
Of the mighty goat
To chant the scores for the chosen
That was lench by the rope
I see the head of the beast
That disguise himself
As the redeemer
Nothing more than the whores of Lilith
As heaven corrupted by it's on blasphemous
Seeds. Just to cause havoc to all
The sons of Hades
The children of the earth whore
Dearest mother.
I want to go where the Rodeo is
I want to go where the Rodeo is
Enchanted the locusts to feed of us all
But what I saw is myself mysteriously fall
Into the pit
Into the pile of shit
Bathing in feces
I'm riding the hounds of hell
Bring watched by the heavens
Trap by the gates of seven

Lustfully
Envious
My taste of Wrath
Eating Glutton souls
My pride to kill you
My passion of greed
To birth my seeds to conquer all
And to adore my slothful sin
You can keep your kingdom
Thy will be fucking done
The Narrator

The Celloist's Unloved Symphony of HIMM

by FD Ravenskraft

The lonesome sound I hear in the Garden as I follow the trails

Of this musical tale

She plays the Dance Macabre

Such a beautiful tune

But the blessing will come soon

As the cello breaths the great doom.

With the beauty of the dark skies.

That already died

As the stones of dead

Their tombs are already read

She's summoning the demons

For a celebration of her concert

The Symphony of the End

As it truly begins. The final sin

The Beauty of The Black Romance

by FD Ravenskraft

With the flower, I bid farewell.

Nothing more to tell you.

My tall tale is done.

My demise has begun

The end of the Twilight's dawn.

My lovers gone

Into the soil that bathed her rotten song.

No more notes to bear

My Death will finally stare.

I'm done in the corrupted affair.

The Gods of all

Welcome us upon the heavenly or hellish stairs

Once Upon A Gluttony
Rose for Mortem Vault

by FD Ravenskraft

Overwhelm with selfish

Needs.

The one who Glutton will bleed

That deluge himself

To the blink of oblivion

The cunning sacrifice

Shredded by the image of fear

As the rose comforts you

To an intervention

To begin your intermission

Without Bn being said

The Veils of The Seer

by FD Ravenskraft Esq. For The Verse of Terror of HIMM

In the lands of thought

And the sight of the wilderness

She will serve you well with secrets unimagine

In the place where darkness dwells

And the Sins she composes on the scriptures of hell

She knows all

And more

Her eyes had no boundaries

In the place she caresses

As she masturbates her soiled finesse

Her test sometimes is the challenging foe

Come to me you fools

Come in in sit I tell you a tale

Of your demise and wit

My hand see all

Thy mind collects

The soul of your

Is mine

With a trade of divine

I told

You're grimly tale

Foretold from the gates of hell

And now the chains

Will trap your soul

For me to manipulate forevermore
Now your story is forever told
As the goddess moon roams
To protect me from the sight of those who seek thee
My veil is my sacred vows
Woe Woe
In the midst of the cold
There's no warm place I'm in the middle of the
Abyss
Dismiss
The Narrator

The De'sade Connection

by FD Ravenskraft

Forgive me as I come to you in ease.

To share my thoughts on the matter of my insanity.

Don't be afraid

I'm only a Poet - The Narrator

In the Master's chamber

The Commander Linger

Into the midst of punishment

His sexual delight

As his lovers live in fright

To only obey his every command

The Complex Passion

Is ruled by the one who hosts

But abusive at his most high

I'm the Sadist Horsemen

I ride through the night

To collect my whores

And ponder them in submission

As I feast from the Cannibal's kitchen

The asylum has bred the population

To lust the filth of all who oppose him

This is so grim

Even my heart melts

The Commander wipes his victims

In the fashion of sodomy

I declare this holiday

A celebration of this curse

As for all things must

Embrace this eternal lust

Obey me or else

The Train of Midnight

by FD Ravenskraft

The midnight train travels in a range

To leave the next stop within the track of deranged

And heading to the dis of hell

As the lost soul is on the board

As the hoards of hell hounds follow to keep them

From escaping their fate

As the gates open and the demon screams in laughter

In the fields of thereafter

The madness is the seeds of pain

As it rains the blood of God's dove

Everyone going insane

As the train stop to rest a bit

The devil sits down to open the bridge of shit

We all know that is doomed

As we assume. We never consume the masses

Of redeem bloom

That curses us all. As the sadist conductor collects

The soul like a bride rapes her groom

As the train begins to reign

On the track of blood

We all gain the sanity of the tears of the angel's rain

The smoke and mirror

Of these lost adores

Being wrap like a consumed murderous whore

As the core of this hard bliss

As the fire of hell kiss

We all will be in the black abyss.

But the train is still rolling, and the reaper stops the track to send

The sinners back

But relax the heavens don't have your back

as the midnight train

Composes its final stop

To dump the souls the river of slop

It made it to its destination

Into the wells of recreation

Nevermore. Hell is your final station

Alas within this common woe

This is your final stop

My door

Tis the season. Your fate is stored

I end this ending

No longer the volume of none

End

Symphony of The Black Baron for HIMM

by FD Ravenskraft

The Wuthering Romance

In a dark glance.

He waits for her for the waltz of the Midnight dance.

His literature of her.

Rewritten as it emerges.

The Casanova of many.

But cherish with her touch

He's the living curse.

Waiting for his love to only realize

She's in the arms of another.

As the black rose cometh.

To summon the play he written

His opera

As the phantom tease.

The immoral disease.

To finally please her love

Death took them both.

As he waits with the rose

That shed the color demise.

His medicine is the milk of her breast

May they both finally rest

The Madness of The Undertaker

By FD Ravenskraft

The midst of the madness of purity

And the darkness is my savior

Coming forth furthermore

Nothing more than a seed of a whore

So soon I have unseen the seen horror

Of all

We have been more than that

That the game has started for the killing of all

I compose this warning of the unseen terror

Alas. The Foolishness of the woe

The emptiness of the soul

Buried alive in the Evening of the dem of hallows

I see myself

But not thyself

An immortal my beloved

Dead and decay

Making love to her corpse

Knowing I will die and hope to lay with her

Forever rotten

Forever coming

I no longer want to.

But to undertake me

The Narrator

In the Beginning There Was the Darkness

by FD Ravenskraft

On the first night

The blackness was still

No sound at all just black

And none not even a single sight

Only the night

The darkness begins to cover the existence

Of sightless fright

Nothing more than a horrible blight

The children were born

The Kraftsmen's kin

Black winged Gods

Spreading the red dawn

As we collect the information

To birth the Raven and crow formation

On the second night

Humans were created to be sacrifice

And feast

But the beast comes from the east comes

To bread out rations

The wolves and lions

And all kind has emerge

To collect and the skies is ours

And the moon shines after

The red harvest song

On the third night

It because a treacherous day

The forbidden light

Where things are beautiful but no so well

Than the dark

After the big bang on us

This is the fall of the light bringer

That curse our lands

This is the beginning of the Gods war

Everything died to be reborn

In the book of Genesis

We survived and the night is still ours

Lucifer curse our lands

As the way we want it

Alas. The Kraftsmen's compose

This last episode

Narrative in code

Beware and behold

Our story unfolds

Fin

Dying love

by FD Ravenskraft

The Day of the blind

Her sweet lips touch mine

Caressing her tongue

Decayed and overdone

Overwhelming and undone

She lurks for the love of another

Covered and

Ready to be discovered

The lust that soothes me so

I love her so long ago

The deceased madame

Needs my love

Like a kiss by the rose of the

Grave

We both behave like a romantic slave

Nothing more shall seize

I made love to her

Before she fade

Her peeling skin begin

To mutilate

As I watched her desperately

Dying separately

From me

I cut out my heart

And lay it beside her

Knowing I'm going to demise

Finally my love we both die

The Theme of The Poisoner

by FD Ravenskraft for The Verses of Terror

The beauty of her lips taste so sweet and tender

That is deadly and warm as I lust for her touch

The foul of my heart is not blessed.

This is my unblessed seed that will

Kill me from her lips the taste of sexual intense

The belly of the goddess the taste of her arsenic

The night caresses the beauty of the season of demise

And I sip the seasoning wine from her breast

The beautiful darkness prevails

The watcher of the night

The Baroness of Mr. Finsternis

The God of Poison

The sour heart of my cold hands bleeds in the frozen abyss

Kiss. kiss

Within the midst of the God of Death

As I swallow my last

The theme of the reaper

Ye Death has come

His summoning his design to collect from this jezebel

To only die by the theme of my own

Born into a thrill that is gone

Dead Letters

by FD Ravenskraft

In The dust of old
And the ancient buried in dust and mold
The letters of the dead
Is being read
So much has to be said
As I compose an haunted dread
For it is read
My soul will take
No longer I shall wake
As the world will know
In this cunning below
This cold fortress
I shall no longer shall linger
I come across the old cellar
Poison in black
To find the bottles of old letters
In the dimmed gloom
That soon we will be doom
I search the graves and every letter
Was there like a penance stare
For me to understand their untamed glory
And the horror that has no story
In this coming flow
Woe
This distress and sorrow
The coming of age
In the days of the Plague Doctor's rage
To collect the dead Letters
And to understand this curse
That forever haunts our souls
Remember those who died
On the days of this fatal show
The world will never know

The Morningstar's Papers

by FD Ravenskraft

Falling from grace
To feast off the human race
To corrupt the souls
Of those to be sold
The ballad of the one
Gods fallen son
Beautiful indeed
Bold into greed
The son of morning
The bringer of light
Now the Twilight of evil
block and unblessed
Signing his contact
Means your doom
Being consume
To your soul is gloom
When you die
Hell will collect
But once you sign yourself
You will pay the piper
For eternality
A place on unkind and pain
As the demons feast
On your flesh no more
Feeling or caress
Fin

The Narrative Monster

by FD Ravenskraft for The Verse of Terror

Ladies and Gentlemen

Welcome to my rhyme

I shall tell you a tale

And you don't have to spend a dime

But only your life. Is worth more

Allow me to open the door

Into a world of nothing more

Than pure horror and Mayhem

No escape my beautiful adore

A word from our sponsor

To sell your soul to me. The monster

And collect your thoughts

And hypnotize your mind

To drain every ounce of your being

Welcome back to the show

You forgotten about me through

But I haven't miss you at all

Just waiting for you to tune in to continue

The story that will unfold

The tall tale heartless glow

The tale has ended

Yes I'm honored to Narrated

And give and take.

Till next time I tell you a tale

Coming from the gates of hell

Till next time

Goodnight

The Hour of the Howling

by FD Ravenskraft for the Verses of Terror

In the storming of midnight,

The moon shines through the night

As all the lands are infected with the Horrors of fright.

In the den of wolves,

She bleeds for the scent of blood

They satisfied her delight

Roaming through the dark woods

As they mate

And the clans don't appreciate the sacrifice

And the exchange to trade

For their love is a blasphemous

In the madness of the corrupted

The vampire will be doomed

As one of theirs

Are in love with the Lycan

War has become a strain on both sides but the lovers are banish

Into the wastelands of the dead

Oh come thee, lover

Let me mate with you

I don't care.

The night is ours

This is the Exitus

To a new beginning

Death shall come to them

In the howling hour

They mate into the banish lands

Of solitude

To caress within the circle of life

Within the Dawn of the pillars

Of night

She spread her Pandora's box

To create the melodies of sin

Only to seed her dearest flesh

To her lover

Their tall tale will embrace the hour

As she moans intensely

In the mourning palace of everlasting

Completes in their favor

Only the howling will tell

The Narrator

The God of the Holocaust for The Mortem of The Omen

by FD Ravenskraft

Upon the broken shores

Of the Gods

One awakens from his slumber from the deep abyss

To curse the events that humans

Has to control this world long enough I shall devour their existence.

Nevermore you Fiends of God

In regard to your failed excuse

To cleans up what was once ours

The lands you bring a harvest

You awaken me

Fools. now allow my rage

Has to control this world long enough I shall devour their existence.

Nevermore you

In the name of the Holocaust

It shall be. Allow me to come through. Mortal filth

The Theater of The Gothic Heart for The Omen of Mortem

by FD Ravenskraft

The Consumed heart

Is a blessed one

Condemned by the promises

Of love and the Damned

Upon the cursive soul

Blessed with love. but protects what's left by all cost

The rottenness of lust

That invades the Virgin's crush

To find it's way to the core

Brokenness

As the sores of Trinity

Adore the chambers of the Black Doors

That opens the heart of the Gothic Amor'

Alas.

May I say Nevermore in the beauty of no more

The Maestro's Sonata for the Mortem Vault

by FD Ravenskraft

He composes the great sonata of her existence. the concerto that blends

And the piano sin. as the melody of her soul is the key to her tune

The maestro caress her, and the rhapsody of her Fatal Opera

The encore of making love to her broken fantasia.

That split his common insanity

With these words, he speaks

My beloved sonata

I compose to thee

Your beloved sinfonia

To glance at your feet

To kiss you. as I finally end this tune with my own

Our Symphony is finally done

The Ballad of the Lycans, for The HIMM Horror

by FD Ravenskraft

You cross my path and you kill my kin

Foolish mortal

You have no need to live

I will consume you and rip your body to oblivion

You call us salvage

We call you the same

On the night of the consume few

On the witching hour, we will hunt

And you will become the haunted

Forever curse in our lands

And your bones collected for rituals we will rule these land

You and vampires alike

Served

The Hollowing of the Lycan for The Mortem Vault

by FD Ravenskraft

His blessed curse

Is his tangled web

In his wolf skin breaths the Lycan's sin

Cleansing the blood from his damned creed

He will cherish his lover

As he knows she afraid of him

He fights for her love

From the fright of his clan

As the moon stuck that faithful

Night. she kissed in his human form

And waited for him on the stroke of midnight

To mate with him in his wolfskin

To bless the howling nights

In the curse of lovemaking, the hollow love awaken

The Symphony of the Plague Orgy for HIMM Vault

by FD Ravenskraft

The Plague of her sex appeal. bleeds out her name

The Goddess of the Babylon race

The beautiful countess of the Snake Waltz

Her lust and needing of you is her blessing into the dark bliss

In the Hungarian Orgy

Feasting in the blood dance. the snake is her beauty

She needs the pleasure. give her your will

To be giving eternal life

Her Damnation is her sexual hell

Never tell your secrets. she knows all

Love maker go to her and become her

The Dancer of the Abyss for the HIMM's Glass

by FD Ravenskraft

In the name of the snake

The blackest take is the soul of her prey

In her waltz of the deep abyss

Her belly hypnotize my lusting for her kiss

She breathes slowly to inhale your energy

Just to get rid of the sinister of me

Needing her and wanting the tongue of Lilith

To release the last of my soul to her

To taste the snake the breeds me

Inside her seed. I'm the Vessel she endures

The Banshee of the Shadow Waltz for the Mortem Vault

by FD Ravenskraft

She's breathing and dance in the motion of a serpent

Beautiful and extremely perfection

To con her victims to watch her as she feeds off their lifespan

In the hands of her own

Only to find her true lover

In the sexual dance of a cunning whore

Your taste for her is bittersweet

To be her slave in the feast of the forbidden

Oil. you will be bathed in her lust

The Children of the Dark Gods

by FD Ravenskraft

The madness within the Garden has been disturb

For the Holiday of the Abyss.

It's the Dance of the Dead

With the host of the Dark Gods.

It's the night that the Delightful ones will rule the Earth with an iron fist.

Humanity is the festival.

There will be sacrifice and devour.

I Reap the Sow of the World's Demise for HIMM

by FD Ravenskraft

I am the inevitable

The existence you always know

But not seen but unseen

To the true light

Of a blinding sight

And now you see

I appear to take you away

To the Garden of many Stone

Where you will lay

And the Baron will come to collect

In the fields of Vowing trees

Where you rest

To be accounted for your time on this

The pity of this planet

I'm the Delightful one

Were the Delightful ones

Alas. Unseen through

But seen not. I reap what you sow

·Breathe no more

The Danse of Requiem for the HIMM

by FD Ravenskraft

The Adagio code of silence

Bleeds the Waltz of Darkness

The Symphony of the Macabre

The Lust of his sound

Cause a deadly bound of Unheavenly

Tune of dark crimson shore

He plays the Danse of Requiem

The strings of the demise

He conducts the orchestra of nature

The screams of the Dead

The hollow choral of Banshee

He is the Reaper with the grim hand

He writes the sinfonia

To end all things from the melodies of the Hourglass

The Stone Garden will rejoice

His Scyth Plays the string of nothing more

The Orgy Anthem of Mortem

by FD Ravenskraft

The Orgy in the House of
Sadist bliss. Composing
The anthology of the Poet's kiss
The Writer forge his cock on her
Pandora's flock.
To unlock the secrets of his creed
That plant his seed
In the season of her Midsummer's
Breed.
As The Psalmist scripture the
Commandments on her breast
His Apprentice rodeo the whore
In the dark night of sodomy
The four bathed in the sweat of the soiled
To honor their pride in a sexual Genocide

The Sands of the HIMORGLASS

by FD Ravenskraft

In the sweet wine of the poisonous divine,

Her sweat broils in the sin of lust.

he endures with his pen

Lovely in between. in the thirst for her touch

In the constant devour of wanting her soul

The oil will bring the scent of the hour and the sands of love

And the black district of the red romance

The tears of her blood he drinks and toasts with the sands of time

As the Baron's darkness thirst for her

The sands will soak in the time of none

Her Mortem love will bondage his exist

The Sands of The HIMORGLASS

by FD Ravenskraft

In the sight of reasoning

I seek the sands of uncanny flow

To rewrite the unwritten

As the darker universe finds light

But the light of a truth sacred sight

In the Hourglass of many

This is the horror that brings the sands of flight

And the blackness of his compose verse

Tells the time and the beginning of the Baron's Grace

To tell the final tales of the end of all

The Wuthering Nights for the Mortem Vault

by FD Ravenskraft

At the castle by the sea
Dreaming the memories
Of the broken. By the Moors
The Season bleeds There
On her Autumn's stare
To feast on the Summer for her lover.
Then the Winter pleases her
On this Wuthering nights. Her
Forbidden Passion.
Only for him to die.
On that Dreaded Spring
As she lay by his grave
To mourn for her loss.
To be a slave to her own insanity
Only the abyss bury her.
To be the voice that forever wails
Naturally

The Hymns of Terror of The HIMM Horror

by FD Ravenskraft

The Smell of the Rain of Blood Scents of the decay reaps

The Airwaves Stench the Old Lands.

Forgotten by the Terror of Death

A Tower of bodies in his wake

Impress by the legend.

To continue the Lover's Quarrel

To end the Supper of Lust

Only to continue

The Horror that is HIMM

The Madame's Horsemen of Mortem

by FD Ravenskraft

My blood. she drinks
The sadist bitch I truly adore
A slave to her will. and only hers
The bondage of a sinner
Untamed and not seize
The Aftermath of Training
Her Commander to Dominate
The servants of her choice
The Mistress he serves
Cunning and bore
Now he's ready to tame them
To please her dearly
Only fearlessly

The Waltz of The Gothikas of Mortem Vault

by FD Ravenskraft

The Waltz of Scars
Broken into pieces by far
In the scenario of scene
The Wedding of the Damned
After a night of forbidden Oil
Bathing in her sweat
In the Dance of the Cursed Opera
She kisses him and caresses his skin
The Gothic Hymns of the lost
The Lover's Paradise
An Unseen Romance never to be
In till death accepts them
An endless end

The Invitation of the Circle of Death for the HIMM Vault

by FD Ravenskraft

Good Evening dear Friends. I'm your host for the Night

Blend in and relax. sit down and be polite for

Your invitation. I choosing for you to come and join

In this delicious delight. in the corner of your chair

Is a cup of refreshment. Tea or Coffee or beverage of choice

Alcohol accept it of course.

The smoke that floats from your cup is your deceitful soul

Brewing with the drops of deadly sweetness

You wondering why now you are paralyzed and stiff

The taste of your beverage is a poisonous intake

Your circle has doomed from the very start

Your cruelty of abuse of writers was your mistake

Pray to your Lord. your soul I shall take. splendid you think

The Omen of Madame Sadist of The Mortem Vault

by FD Ravenskraft

The Queen of the eternal Damned
Embark on her sacrificial lambs
In the mirror of a unmask. she feeds off your lust
And you come closer. The Madame
The Whore of Babylon's scorn. her satisfied hunger
For sodomy and bondage Mortem.
Come a little closer. and taste her lips
Your Endless Omen

The Pillars of Father Gothic from the HIMM Horror

by FD Ravenskraft

The Dimmed shadows rain on his accord Horror
To seek his nature.
Being wrongfully murdered for his blasphemous
Pen by his cunning righteous foes.
He forges his rage in the night of woe.
They will reap what they sow.
To meet their end in his fatal flow

The Symphony of Sierra's Sadism

by FD Ravenskraft

She breathes the broken tune
His symphony unheard and not so known
But he composes the finished score
In the asylum where the dark soprano
Voice the Mortem song.
The Raven's Quartet
The Horror Ignites. The Master's beloved delight
She rewrites his concerto. with her gothic tone
Nothing more, her forbidden shore

The Raven in the Spider's Den

by FD Ravenskraft

I bleed out the rivers of blood

And drink the venom of spiders

And as I dine with my kind

In the Crow's den

Caressing the Ravens blessed sin

I am one man

That live the traits of horror

The poet that eats the souls of his pen

Drinking the poison that leaks out his own

I am what I am

Nothing more

The Feast of The Gods

by FD Ravenskraft

My brothers. join me once more
In the hordes of the deep
To feed on the fiends of humans
Their sins have broken
The reality of their conscious minds
To bleed summoning of us
The Gods will feed
We will indeed, devour your Creed
And swallow your souls
You have open the doors to your doom
Yes, it is coming and soon.
In the name of us all

The coming of the Strawmen (The Final Conflict for The Omen of HIMM)

by FD Ravenskraft

I will cut this short
This is the end for all
My brothers will assemble
From the depths of the abyss
We are the madness
Within. and the sins of many
We're coming for you
And only you
Humanity will end
We are the children of the harvest
Your lives will be consume
From every field
You will be buried in the garden
Of soil. this is the end of the
Beginning of all

The Affair of The Reaper's Stare for HIMM

by FD Ravenskraft

A Countless bliss

Ends with a Tis

A season of hell

As the reaper impaled

Constantly embrace

The ending of the human race.

Even he has a holiday

Of his own accord.

To make love to his Decayed lover.

Like no other.

He records through the hourglass

Of time.

Just to lay with her

His immortal crime.

Is neglecting his demise

As hell is angry

And heaven are in rage.

That the deadline of all

Spirits

Is delayed.

She plead with him

He kisses her dearly.

The nightmare of dream

Is nearly complete.

The reaper's is now

Along with bride.

The will to conquer

Time will decide.

The Shattered Heart for HIMM

by FD Ravenskraft

In the mirror of drowning blood

She embraces the lust of her image

To find out she doesn't have a heart

Until she realize there was no beat to hear

She was caught not knowing

That the mirror is heart

She sees herself only with a hand

Saying here. I took it

Because you don't know how to use it

Until she's ready to accept

That being cold is a lonely place

She refuse and died in front of herself

The mirror claim her

To be imprisoned as her body decay from existence

Ashes to ashes

Dust to ruins

Death See All for HIMM

by FD Ravenskraft

I see things in rhythm and compose my thoughts

To take the time to focus on the lives that are bought

By the Kings and Queens of the living.

Now I bought them with my scythe to collect their souls

And sale them to the abyss of hell

You never cheat the living for the lives you take

I'm the Reaper waiting

And waiting for my moment to create the scene

Now you shake. because I'm coming for you

I'm the ruler and the demise

Now you will die for your common lies

Your soul will not be

But lock up in Hell's Divine

Except you burn for your crimes

The Shades of a Touch for HIMM

by FD Ravenskraft

The Ghostly caress within

It's an unloved symphony. He whispering

The rhyme to his beloved

Valentine. The grasp of his cold image

Frozen in time

He was a victim of a crime

Of the forbidden lust

Now the wraith is in love

With his dead lover's ancestor

She enters the chamber of the untamed ghost

Just to relive that moment from her past

She will die on his Ghostly arms

To join him in Death

The Chessboard Conspiracy

by FD Ravenskraft

In the hours of your final scene
You wake up in your nightly dreams
Afraid to commit in this game it seems
You need to focus on me and your pieces
To be redeemed
But of course, I noticed your fading slowly
Into the abyss boy
Either way, you can't record
That is already been accord
Beware that you're mine.
Checkmate. My shiny rhyme

The Black Queen of Babylon

by FD Ravenskraft

The beauty of the beast.
the dark Babylon whore
Ss scorned for her lust for men.
but we see the cats wouldn't allow
Her to be in touch
Her soul belongs to them.
Every man is devoured as they want satisfaction
The night belongs to her
As their cats eat the leftovers she didn't finish.
Collect the bones and the remains of her victims
Only to lust for more.
But soon it's going to end her

The Sinful Case of the Soiled Dove

by FD Ravenskraft

When death comes for her

The deal for her sins is not to die

But not to live either.

But a walking corpse that is tamed by her ghostly wraith.

The body count of the bad men

That she had intercourse with is her downfall.

The cruelty of good men brought her here in the form of lusting fear.

Now she sees her tortured self

Consume spirits of the dead.

As hell awaits for her when she's finally full

The Gothmother's Affair

by FD Ravenskraft

They both dance till midnight.

As the winds come from both of their lusting kisses

To bear witness to their grasping caress

Known to those the affair of the Dark Gods

Love me. she said

But he replied the darkness is my true love

And that is you. they both made love in the shades of blood

Only to bear the world to their will

The Black Opera

by FD Ravenskraft

We see here in our dreams on a Dark Holiday
As it seems that the soprano lust for a tune
To be heard by the world. the bleeding heart of hers
Cometh to consume the hearts of the crowd
On this Christmas Eve.
The dark caroling shall be the doom of us all
The Gothic Siren shall roar

Ravenskraft

Presents

The Mortem Vault of HIMM's Omen

The Hidden Collection of Terror

When you look into the hourglass you will see the nightmares. Within the glass of terror. He is the Master of Mayhem!

- *HIMM*